This book belongs to

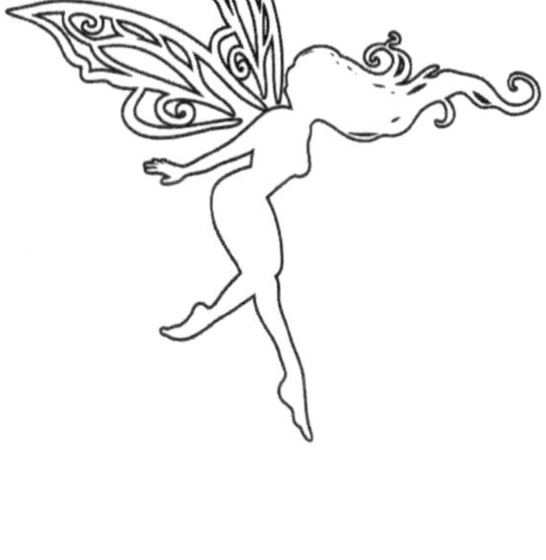

Includes 2 each of 25 Grayscale Fantasy Forests coloring images by Selina Fenech.

As an artist, color is a thing of magic in my life. Color creates shapes, forms, and feelings in the artworks I paint. Laying color onto a blank page is when I feel closest to true magic, when I feel happiest and most relaxed, and it's through what I create that I share my love of magic with the world. Through my coloring books I want to share that same magic with you.

The artworks in this book are black and white versions optimized for coloring of my original paintings which I have painted over the last ten years as a professional artist.

When designing my books I decided to print them with two copies of each design, because as an artist I know there are always so many possibilities! I also wanted to give everybody the chance of a do-over with every design in case of an oops (as an artist I know that happens too!). Try a different medium, or a different colour scheme. Or share the magic with a friend or family member. Because sharing your creativity and joy of color is the best magic of all. ~ *Selina*

See the colors the artist chose for her paintings at www.selinafenech.com

Never run out of fantasy coloring pages by signing up to Selina's newsletter. Get free downloadable pages and updates on new books at - selinafenech.com/free-coloring-sampler/

Enchanted Magical Forests - Grayscale Coloring Edition

by Selina Fenech

First Published September 2016

Published by Fairies and Fantasy PTY LTD

ISBN: 978-0-9945852-4-0

Grayscale Edition Coloring Book

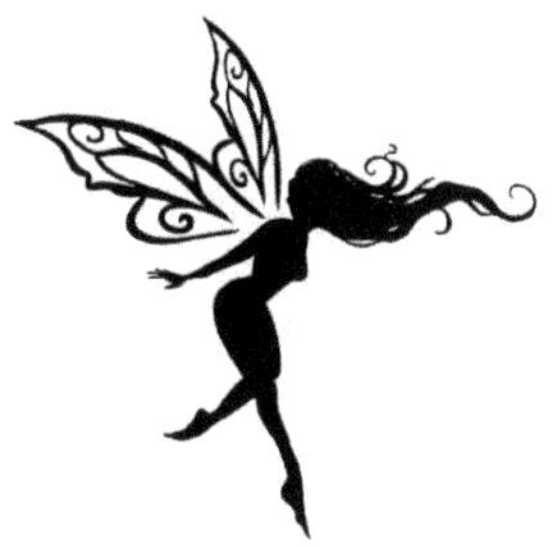

Unlike A Traditional Coloring Book...

Grayscale coloring offers a different coloring experience than normal outlined designs. Coloring over a grayscale artwork where the tonal values are already in place means most of the shading has been done for you, creating much richer final creations like magic.

How Does Grayscale Coloring Work?

Begin by coloring a single color over an entire area, just as you would fill a blank space in a traditional coloring book, and the grayscale image underneath does the work of shading for you. Advanced colorists can use the grayscale artwork as a guide to layering their own choices of light and dark colors.

Tips...

- There is no right or wrong way to color, and with two of each image, there's no pressure.
- This book works best with color pencils, pastels, or markers.
- Slip a piece of card behind the image you're working on in case the markers bleed through.
- Don't be scared to dismantle this book. Cut finished pages out to frame, or split the book in half where the second set of images start so you and a loved one can color together.
- If you coloring pencils or mediums are too opaque and are covering up the grayscale image too much, practice varying how heavily you apply them. Sometimes you may need them thicker in the darker areas, and sometimes you might need them thinner, allowing more black to show through, depending on the color you are using.
- Work from dark to light. Lighter pencils can be waxy and prevent darker colors holding, and using light last over darker colours will help blend them together.
- Always keep your pencils well sharpened, you'll get better results with less effort.
- Try picking a light, medium, and dark color for each area and use the grayscale image as a guide for where to place them. The three shades don't need to be the same color, for example, try lemon yellow for light areas, orange for medium, and purple for shadows. This is a great combination for skin.

“Autumn Slumber”

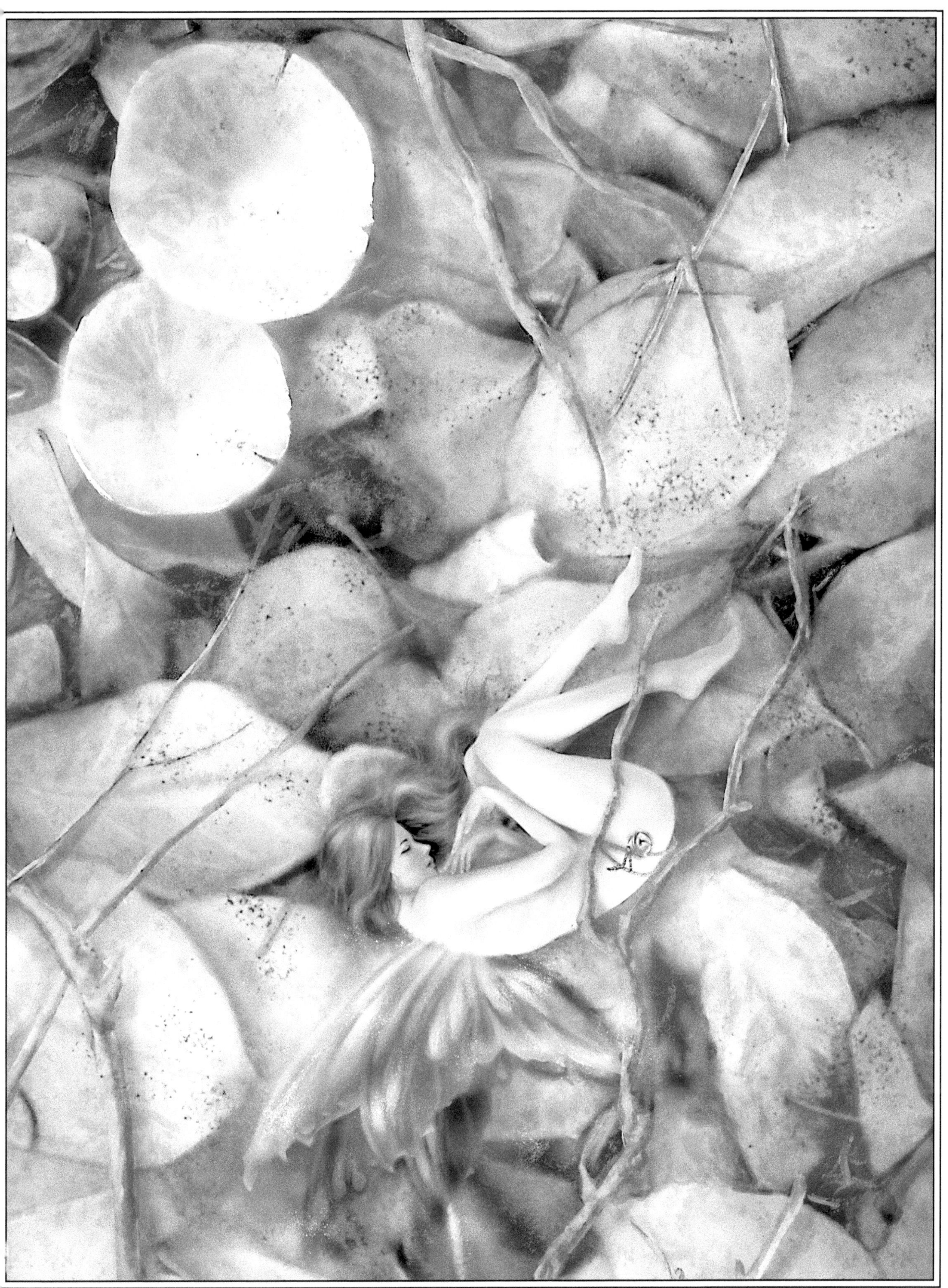

"To Meet a Dragon"

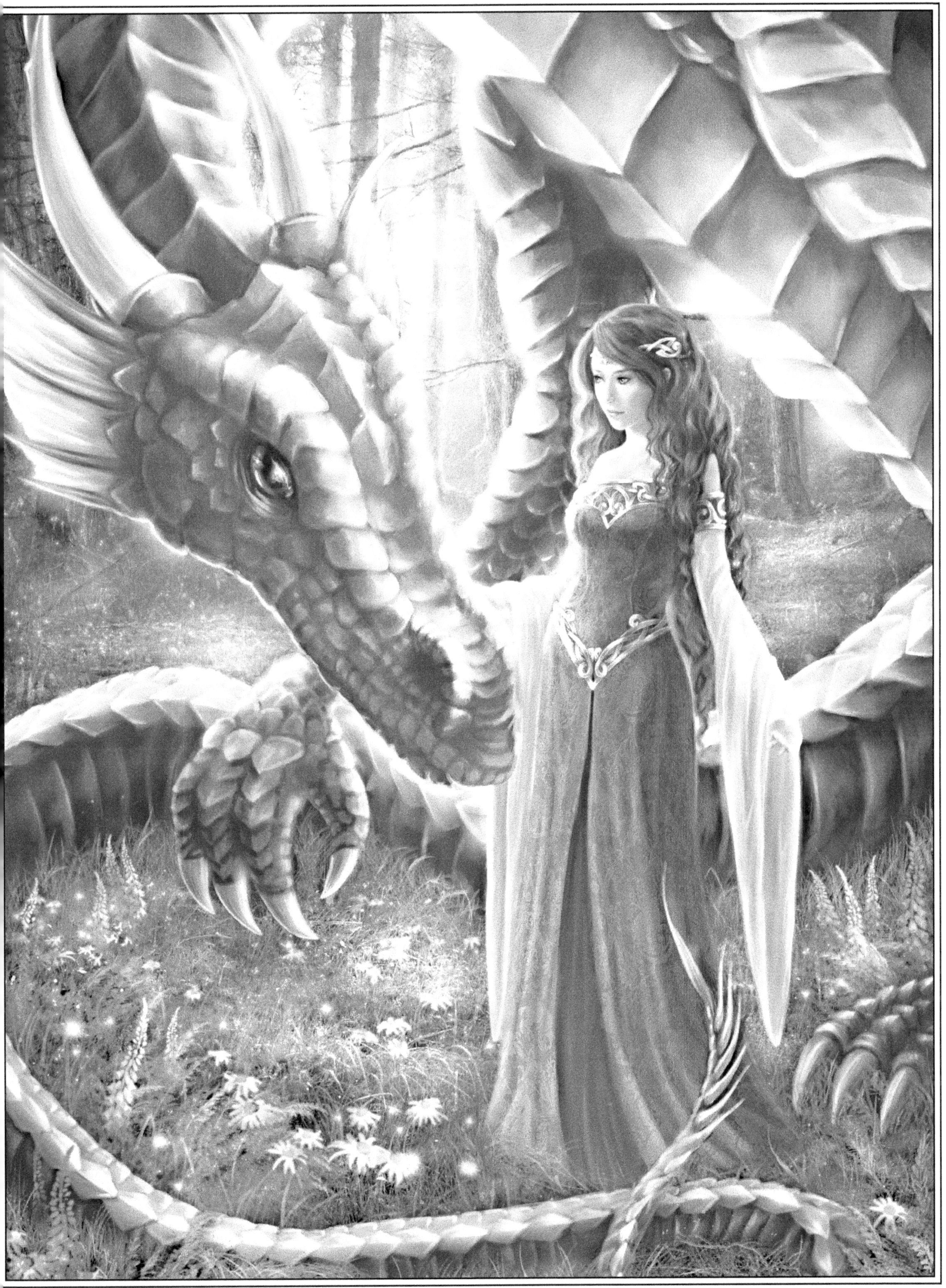

“Hatchling”

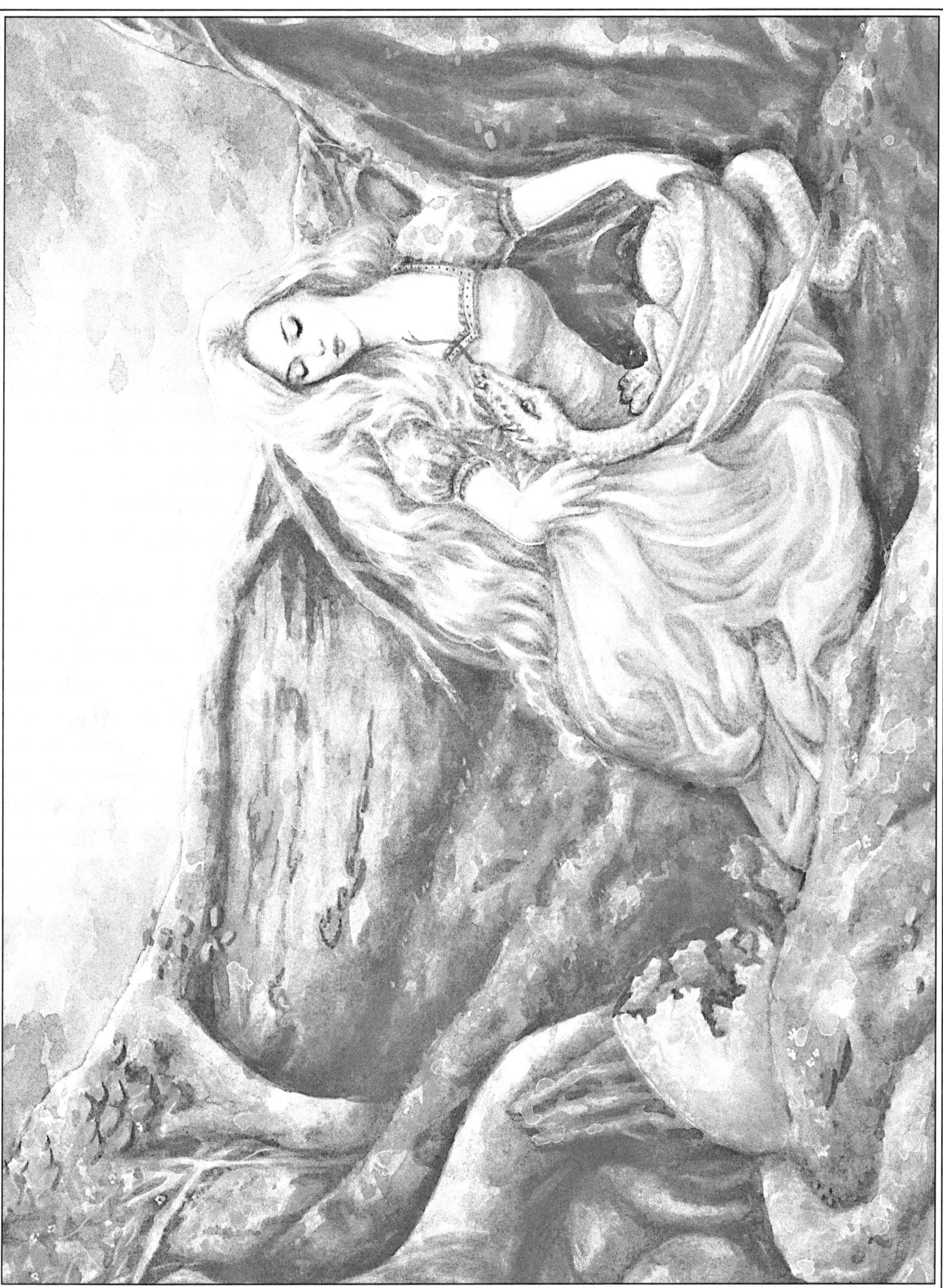

"Twilight Stroll"

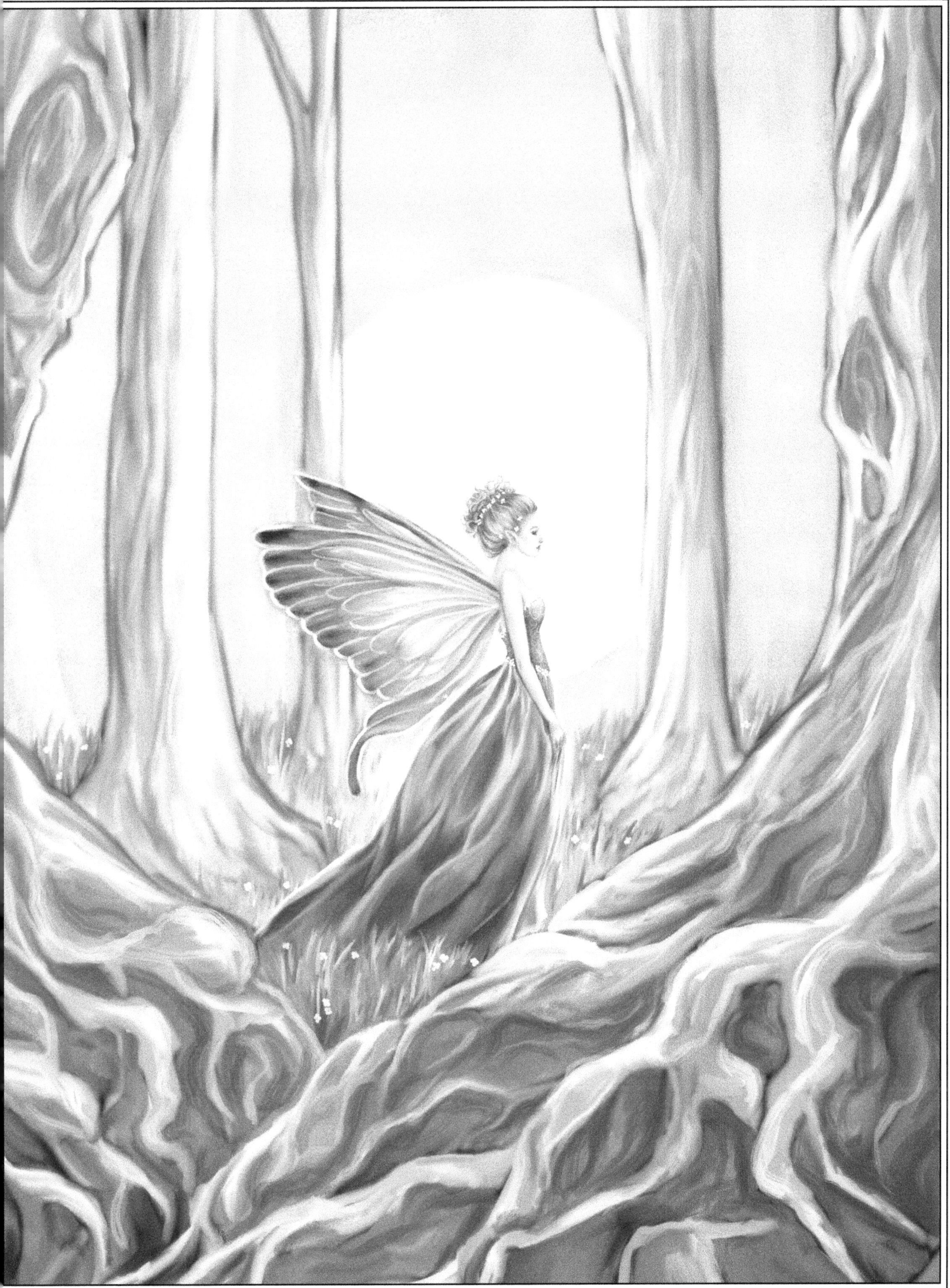

"Along the Forest Path"

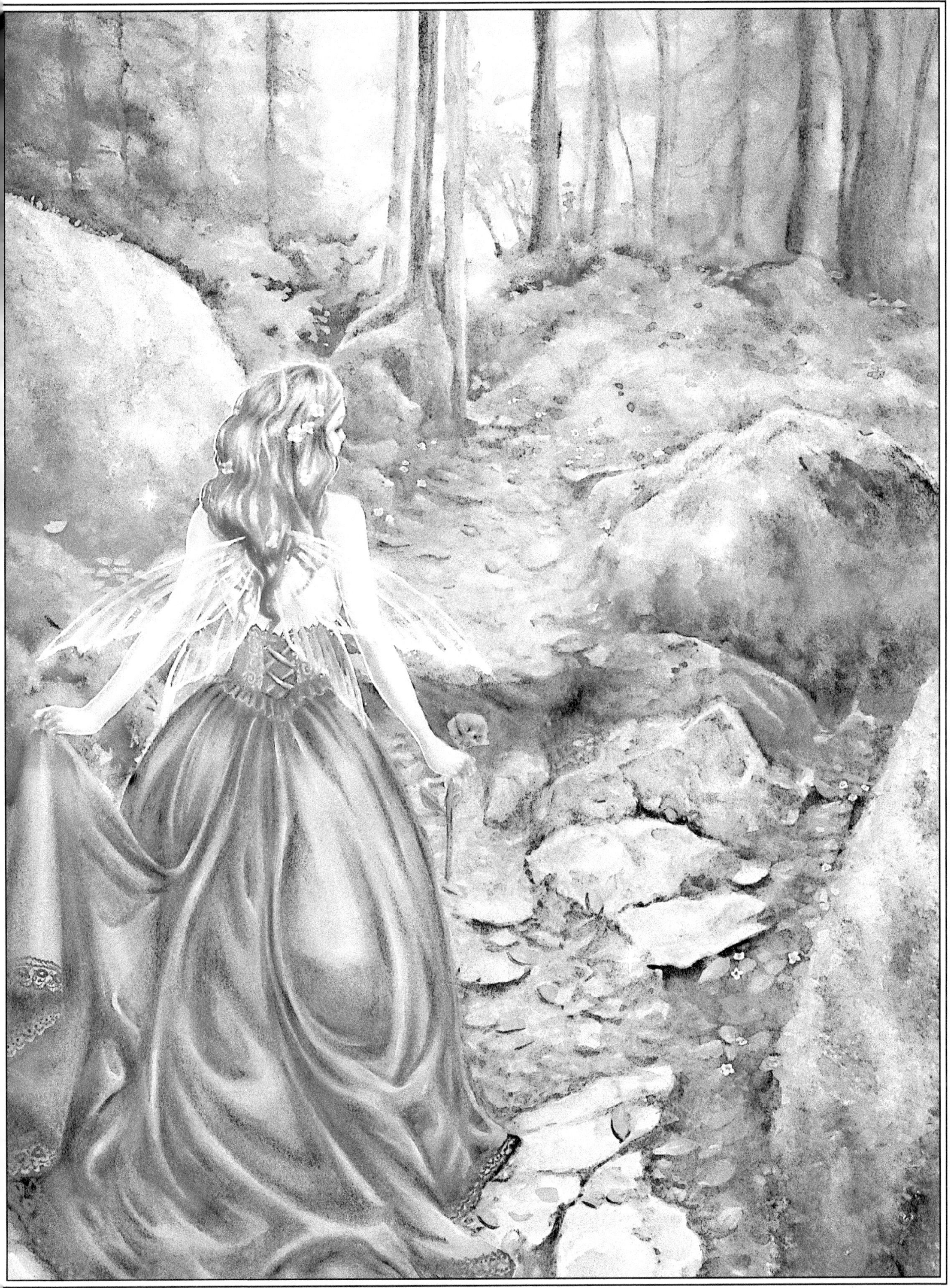

"Blodeuwedd in Bloom"

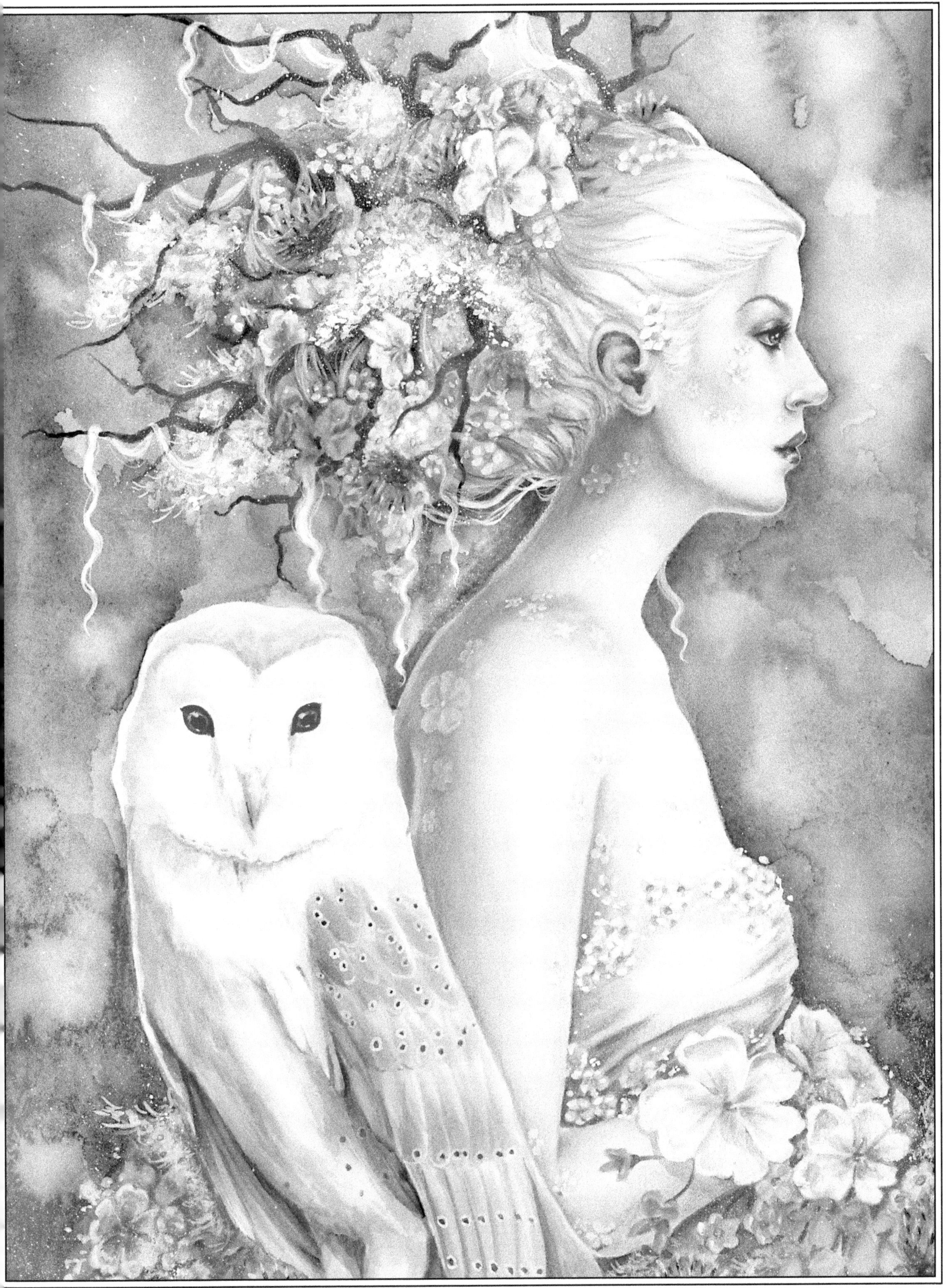

"Dance of the Graces"

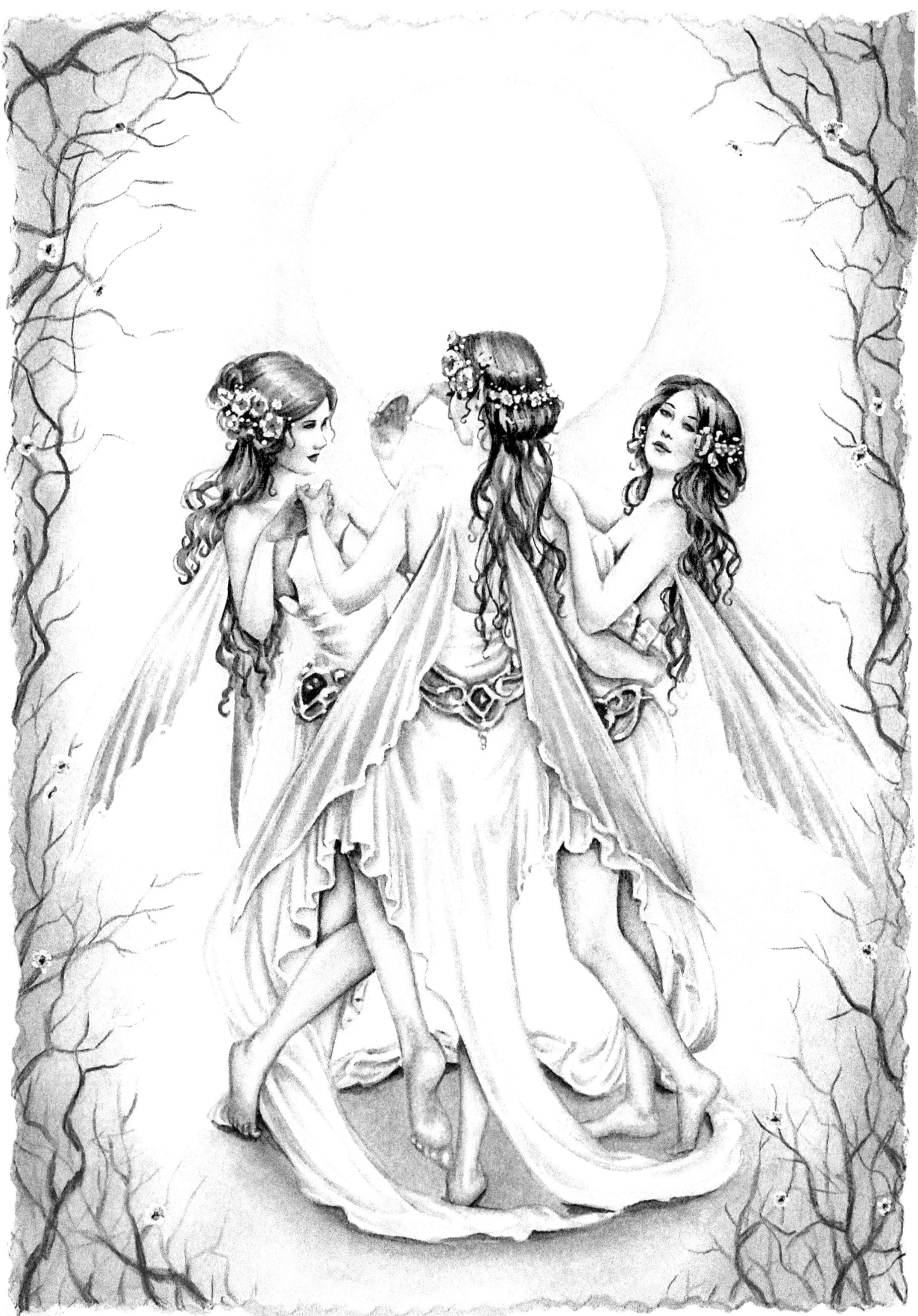

"Earth, Life, Magic"

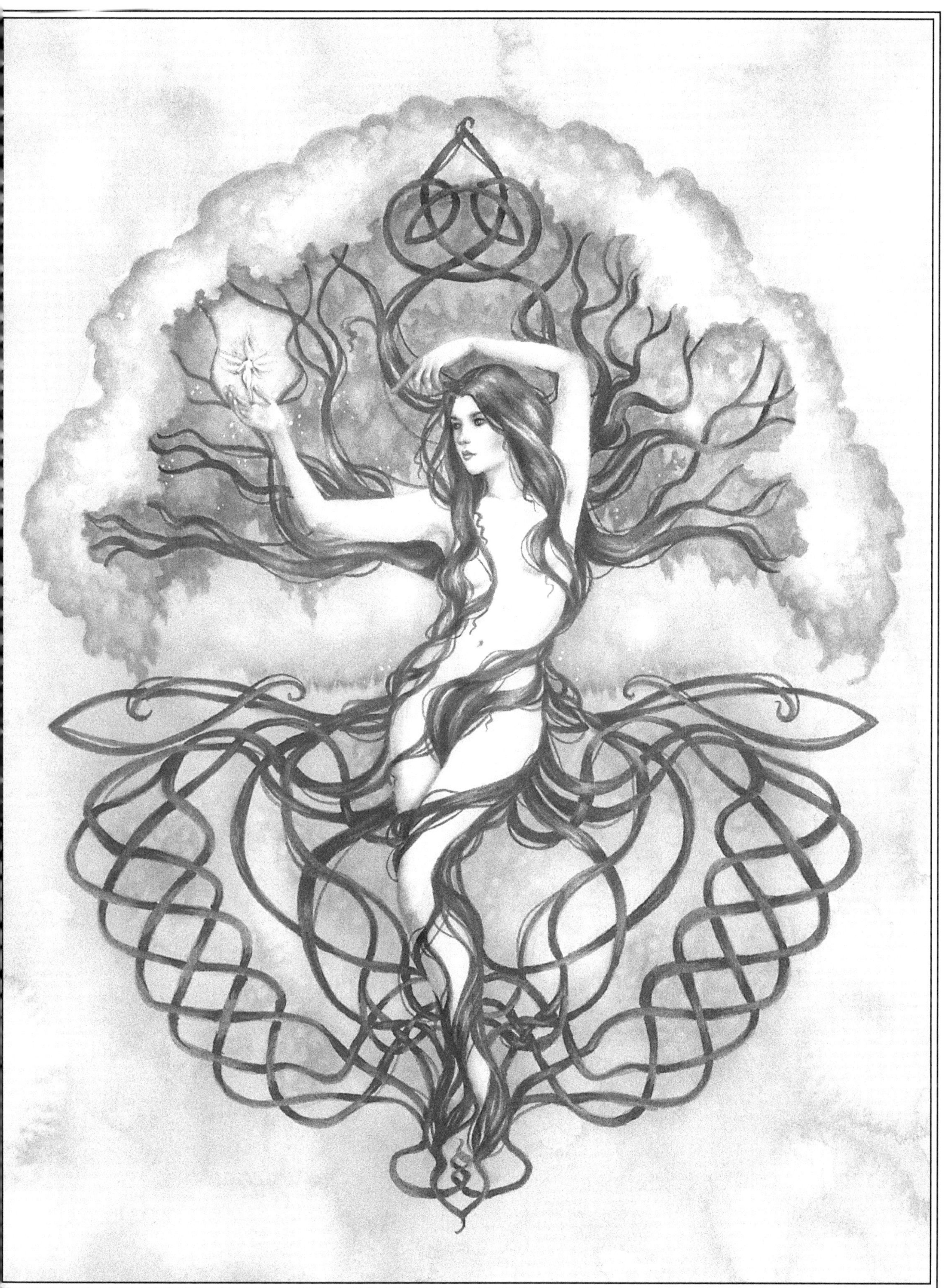

"Moonlit Kiss"

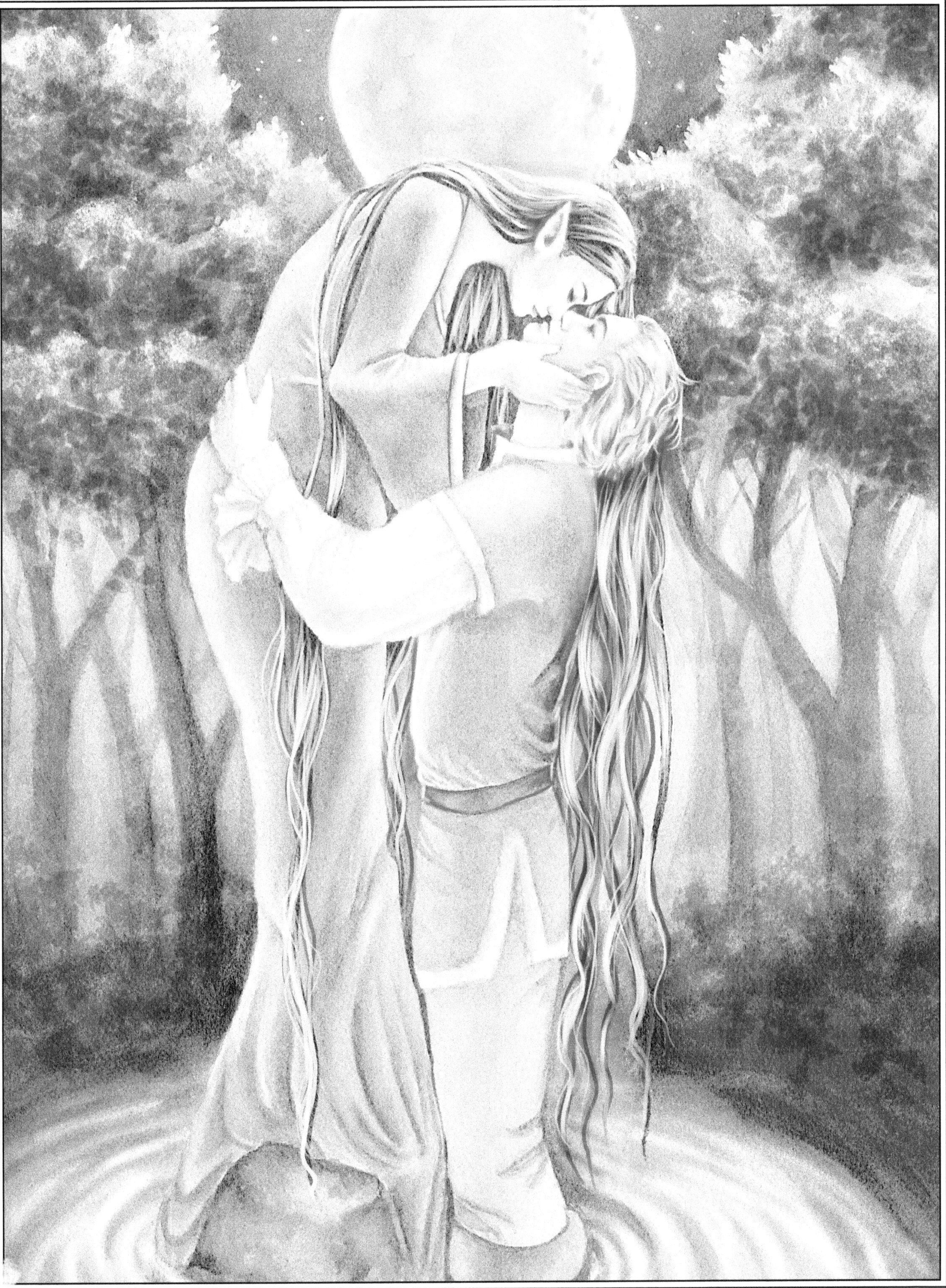

"Fairy Wishing Well"

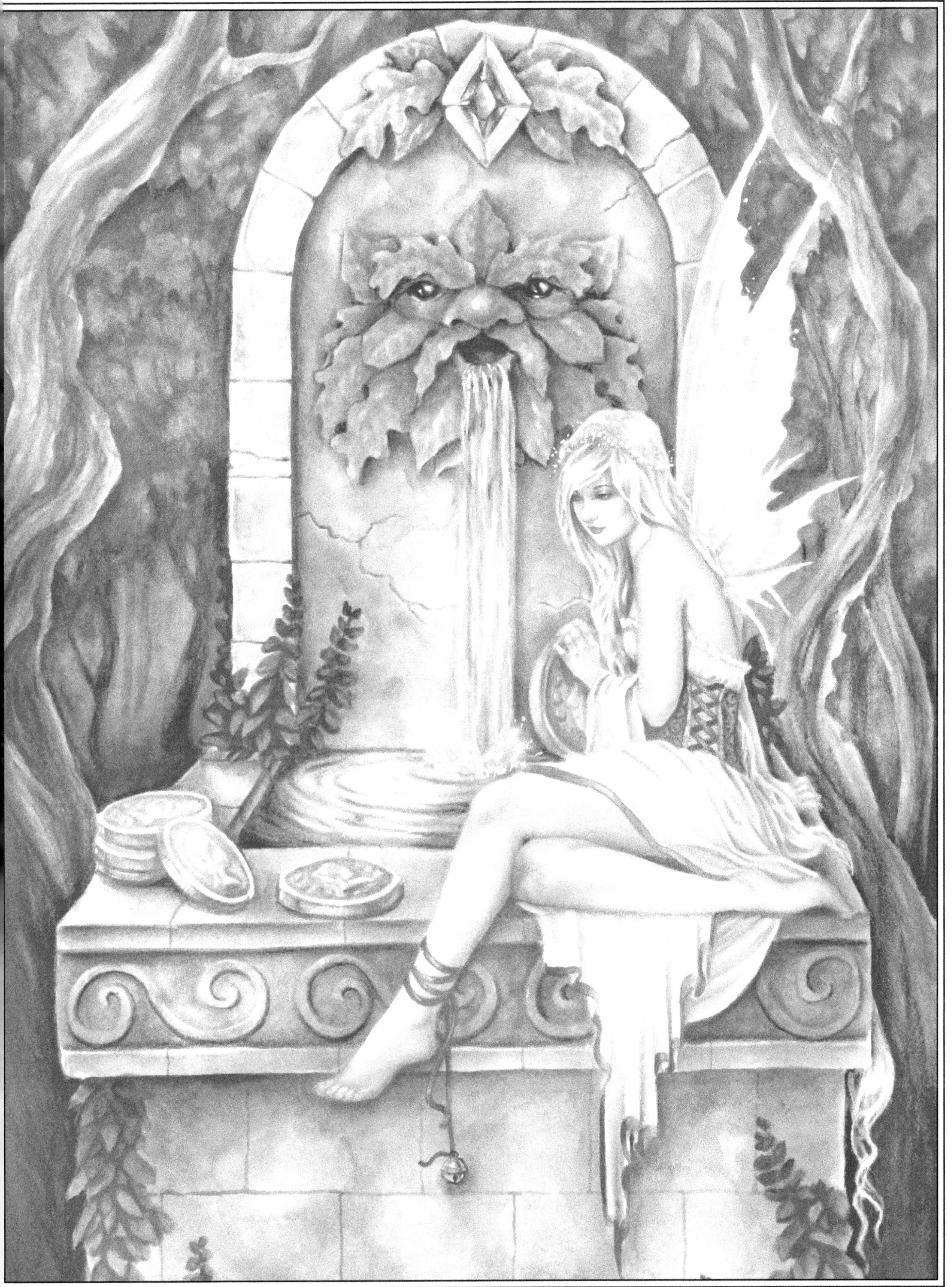

"Glimpse"

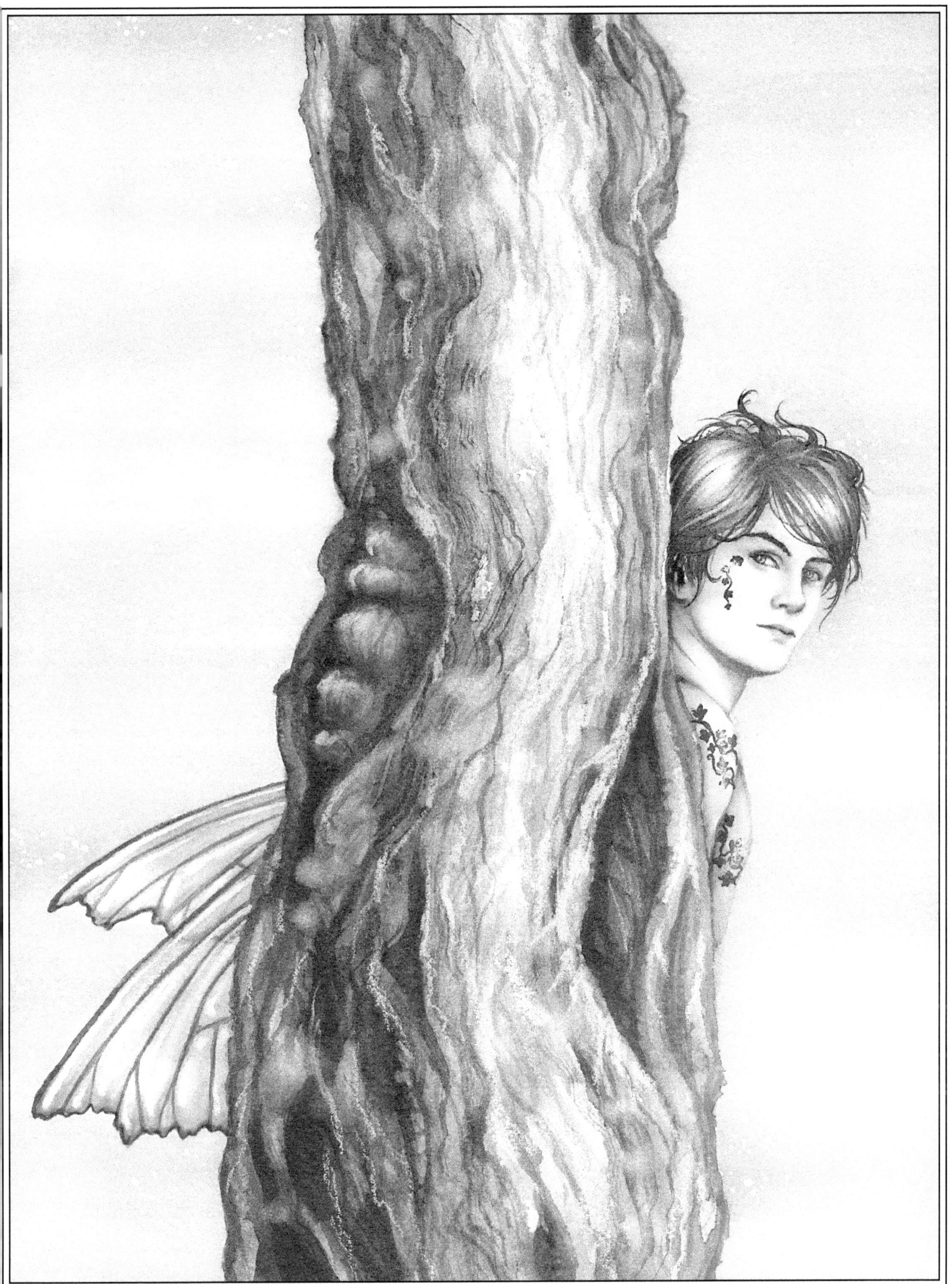

"Hide and Seek"

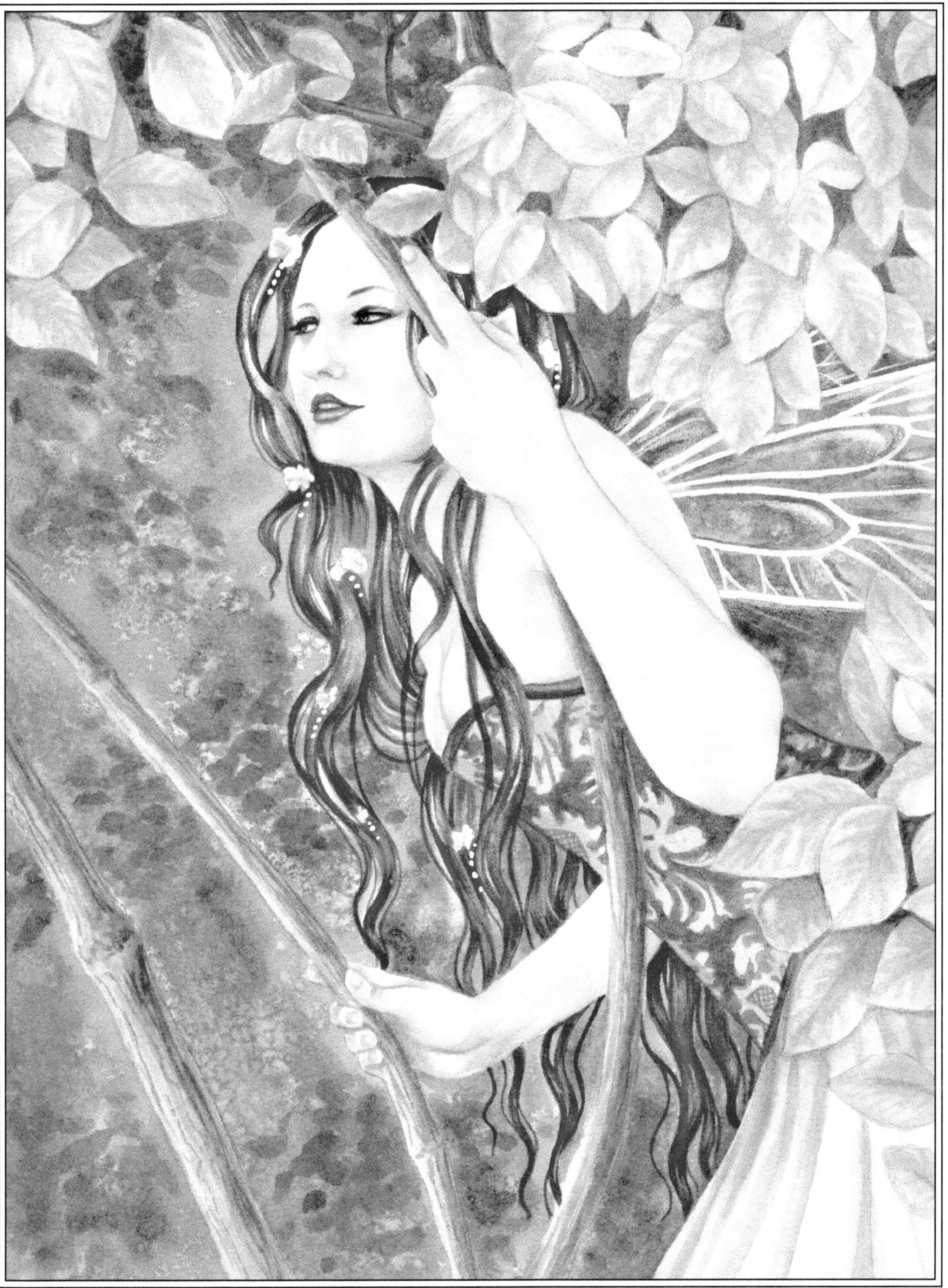

"Into the Woods"

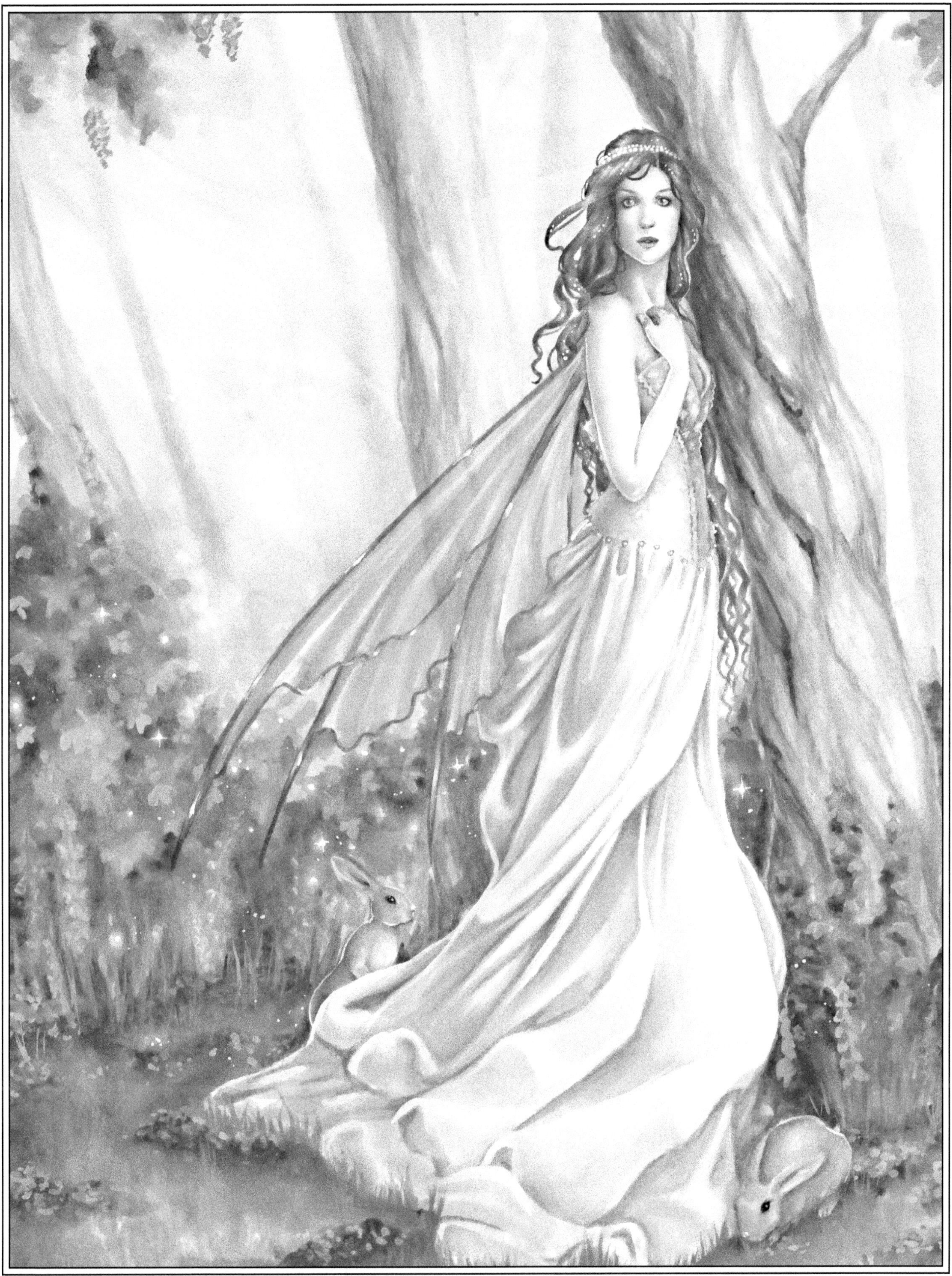

"Kindred"

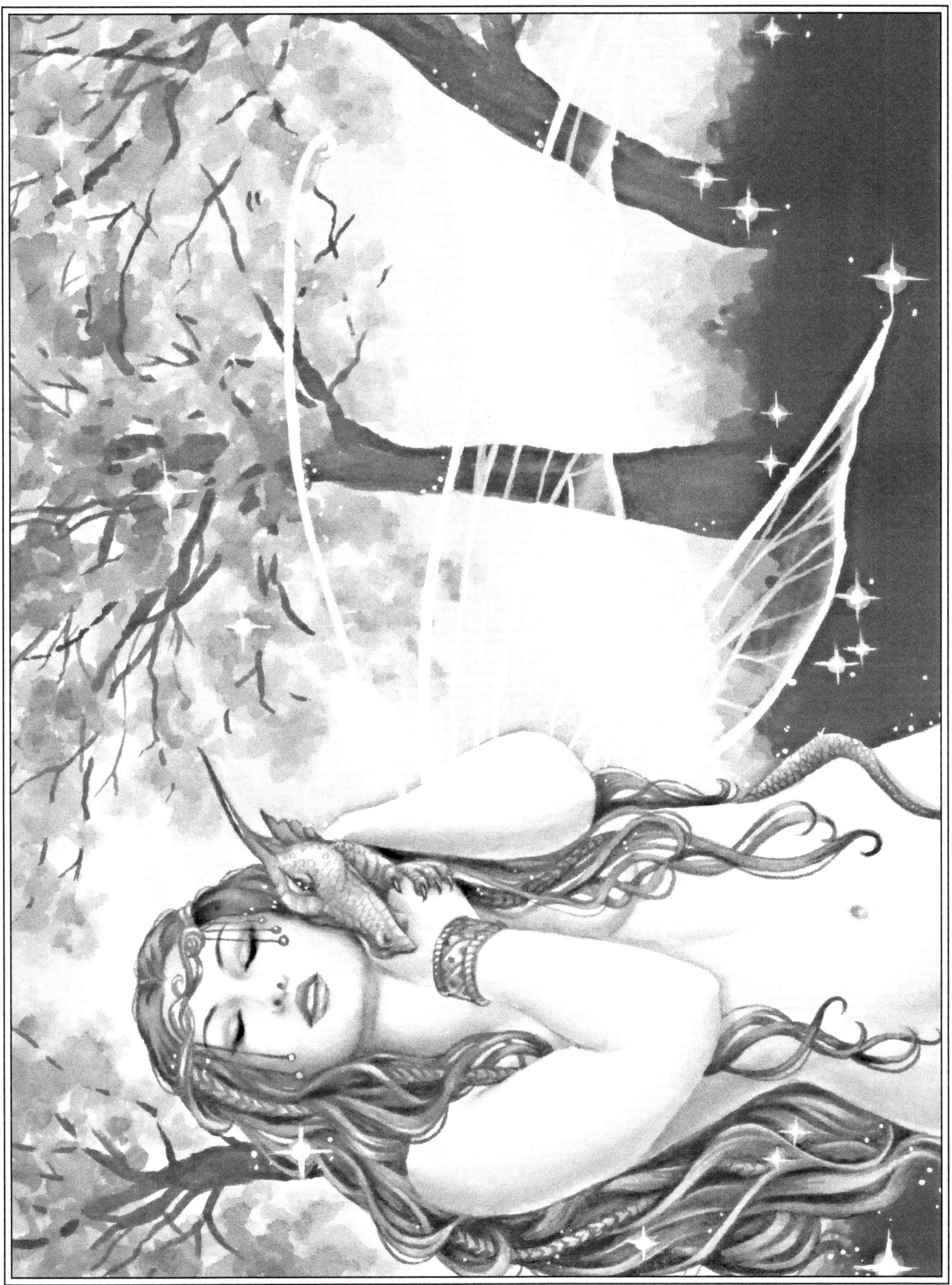

"Lilac Magic"

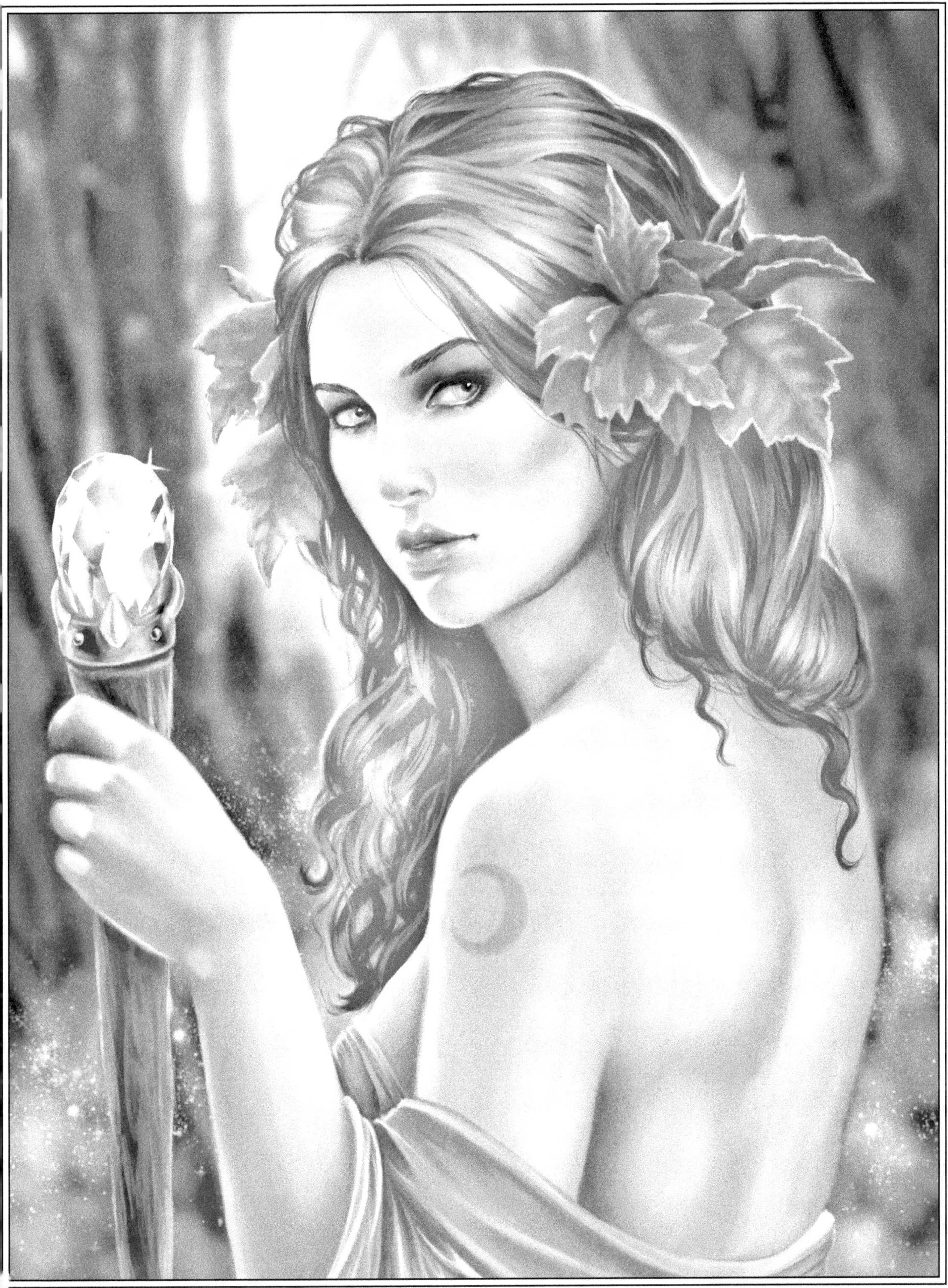

"Magic and Moonlight"

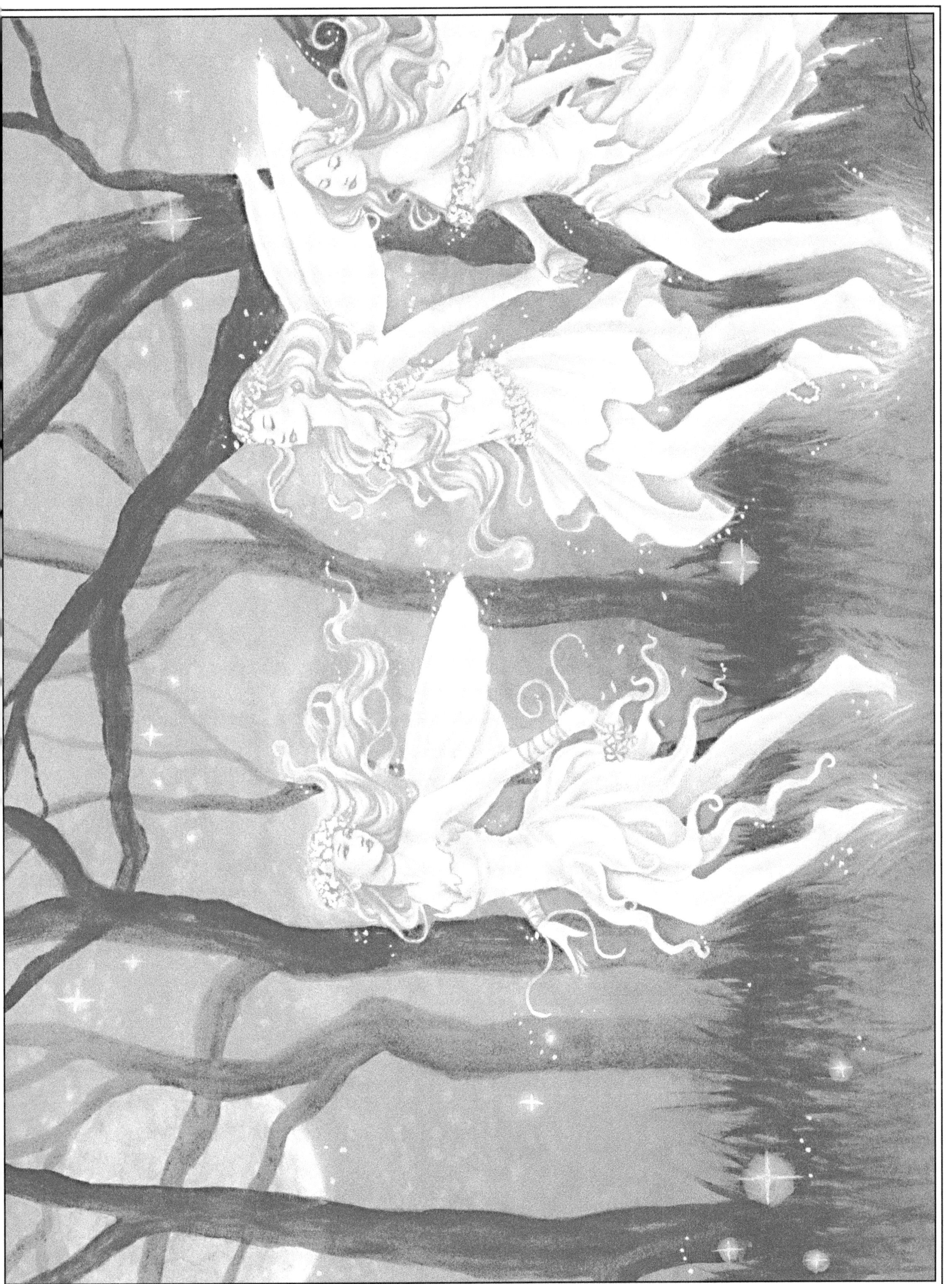

"Morgana's Secret"

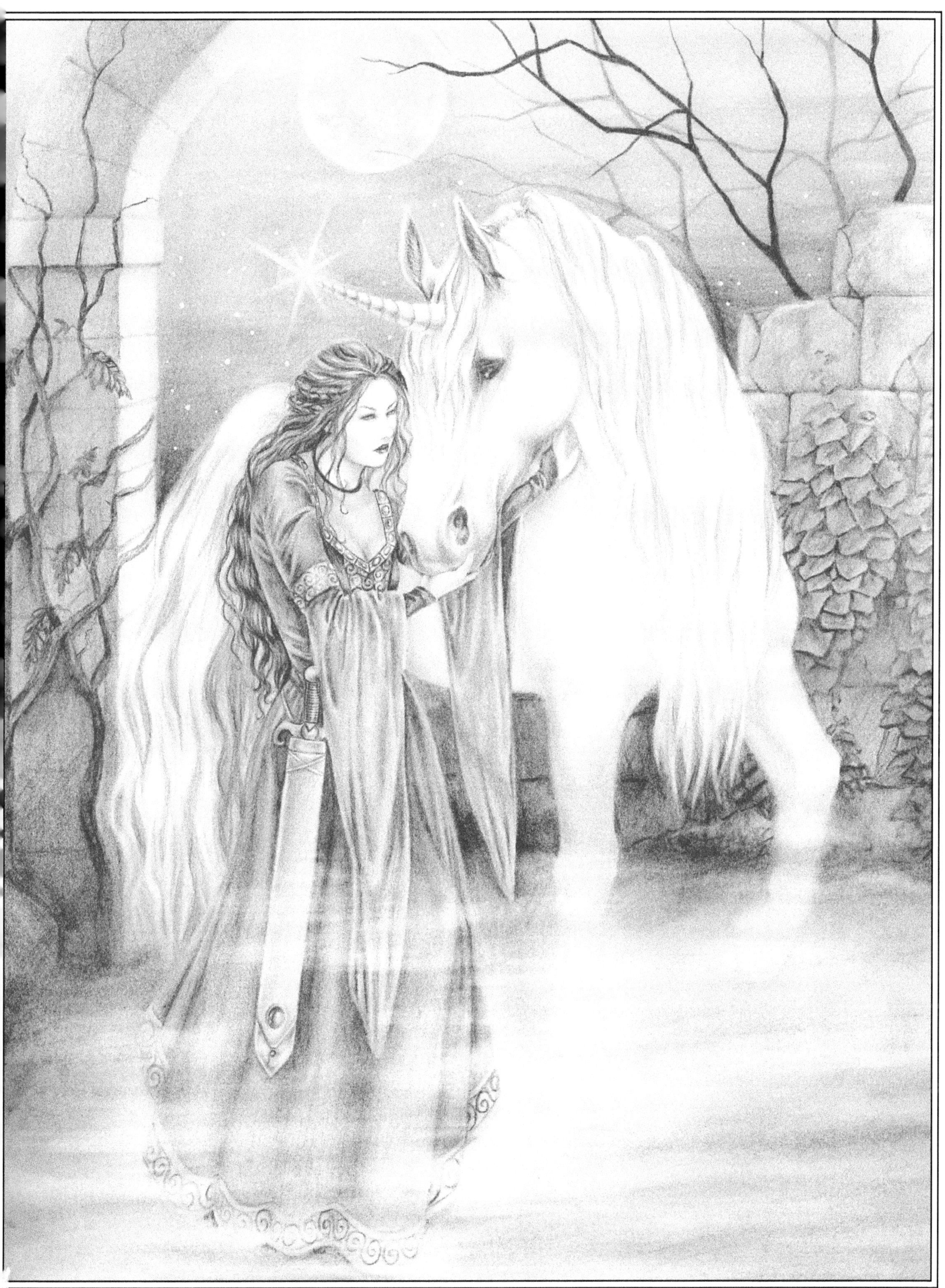

"Ravenkin"

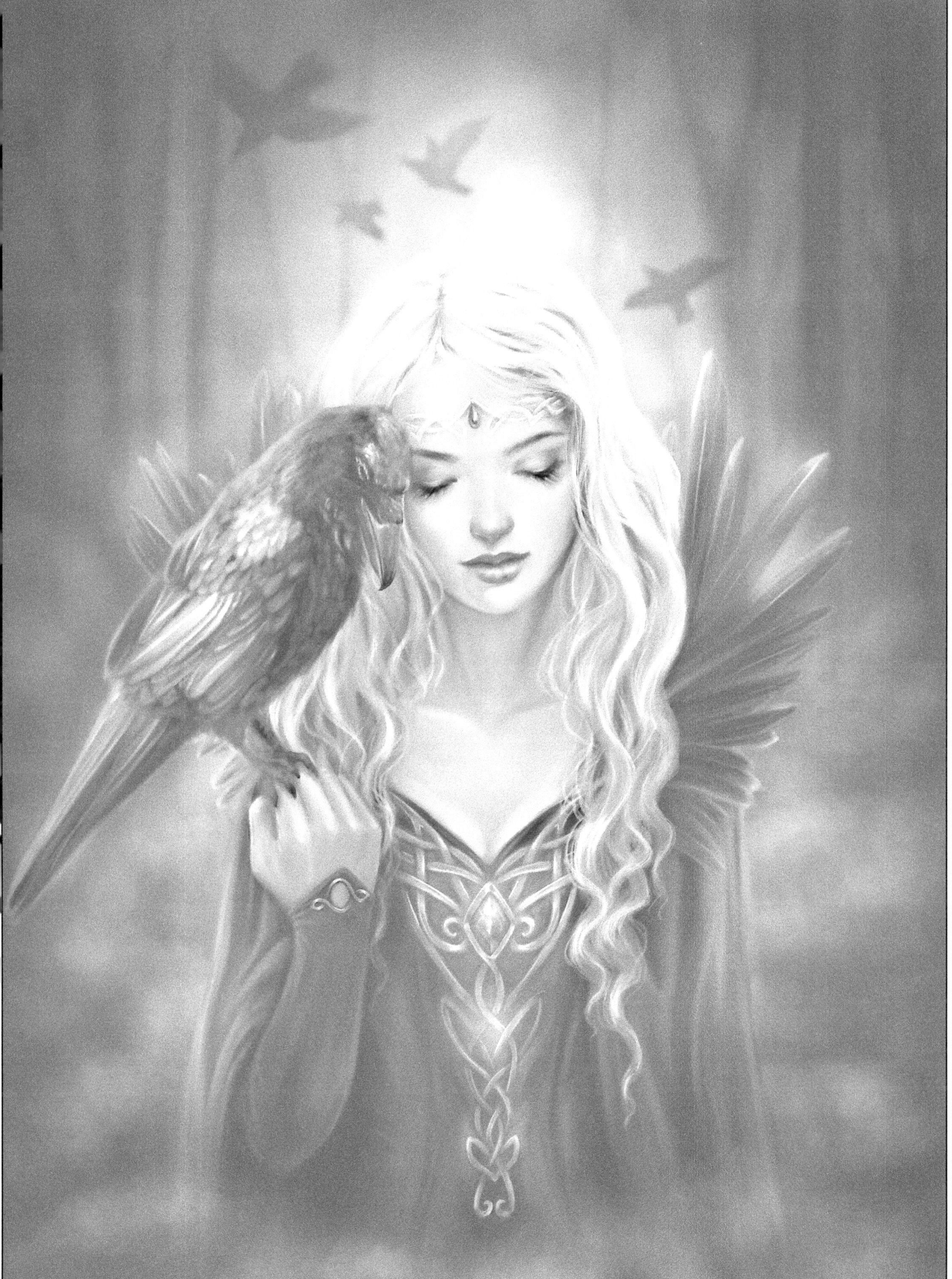

“Rockabye”

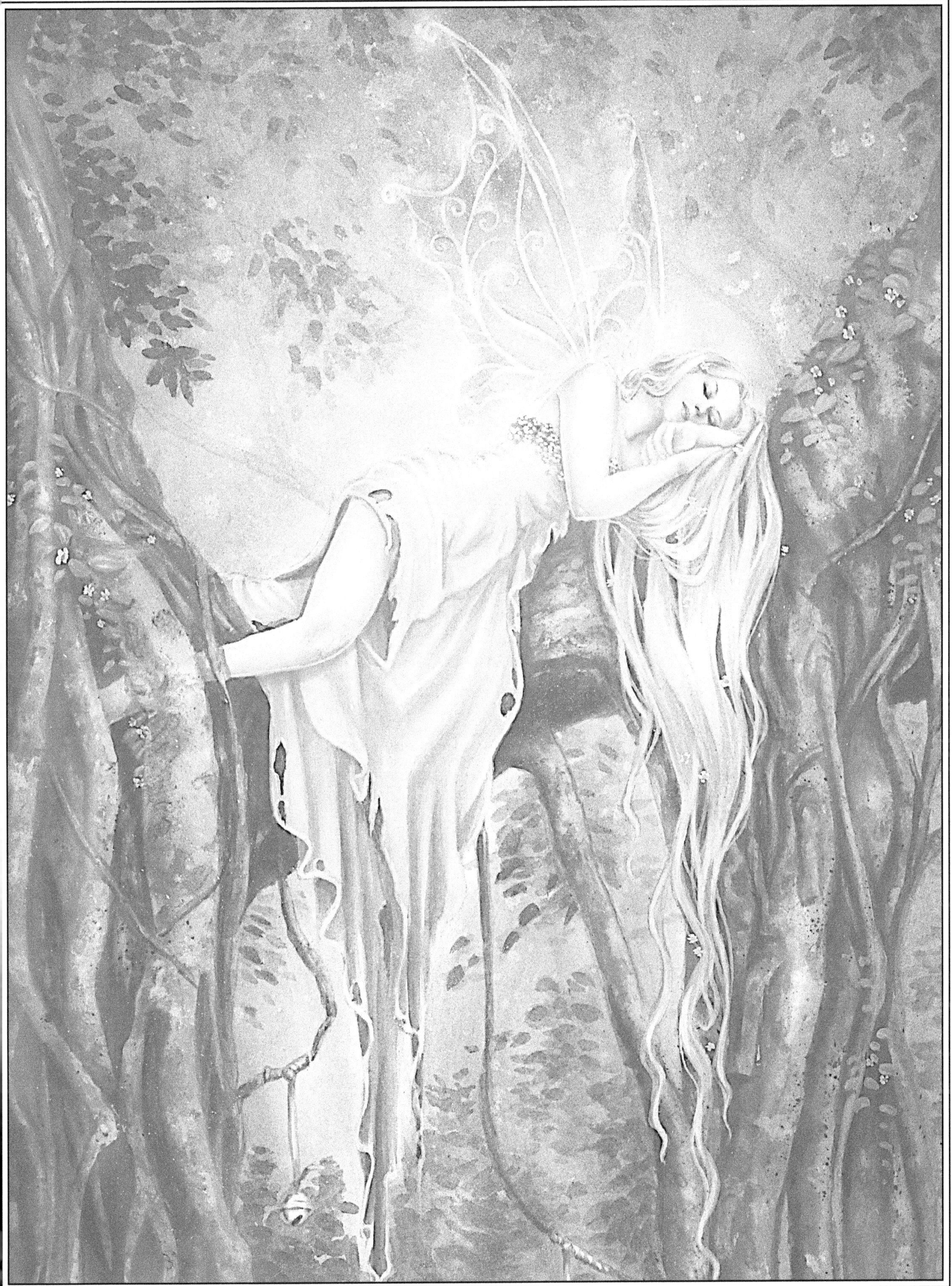

"Secret Doorway"

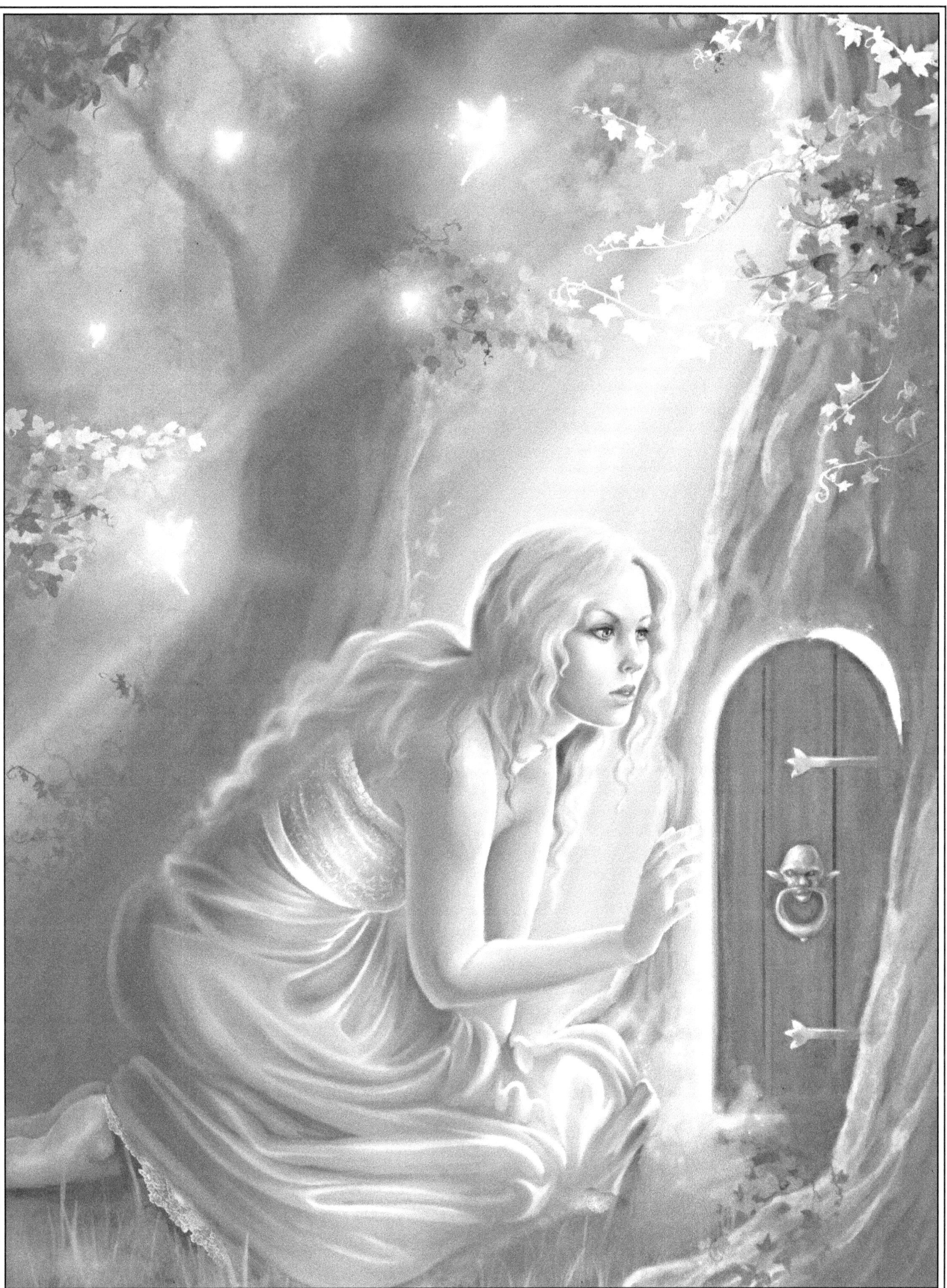

"Sleepy Spring"

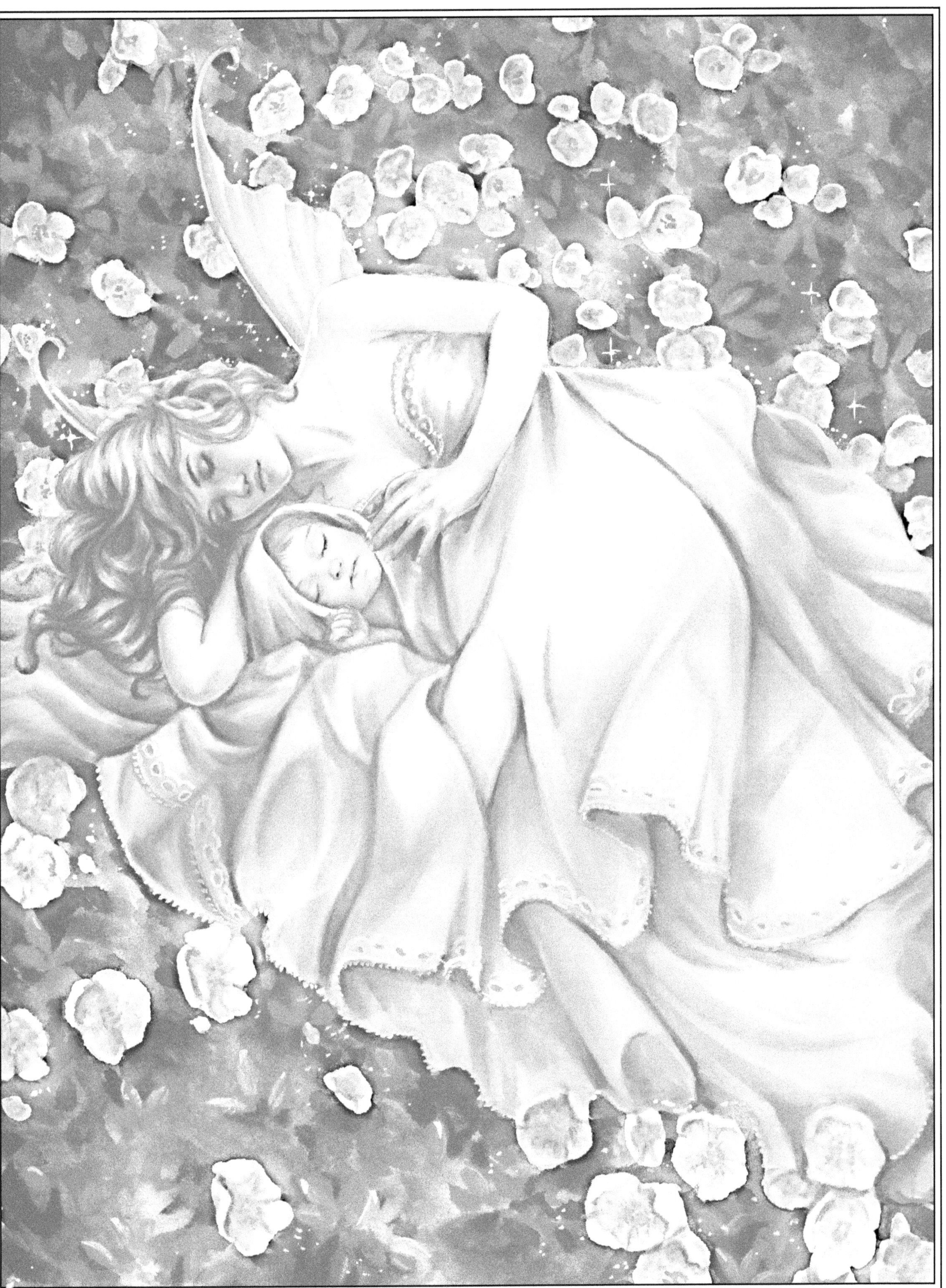

"Nature's Magic"

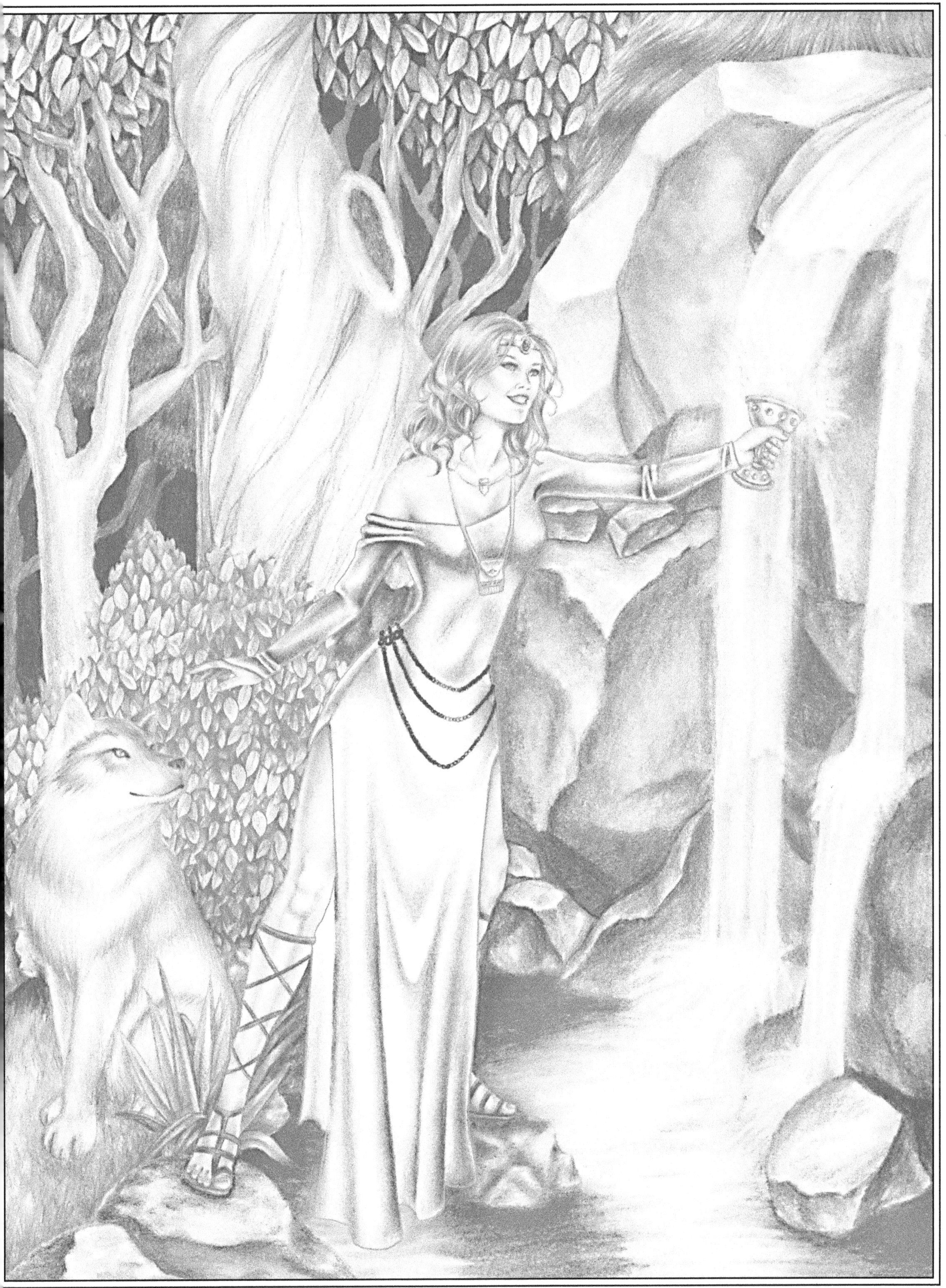

"Vila - Nature's Angel"

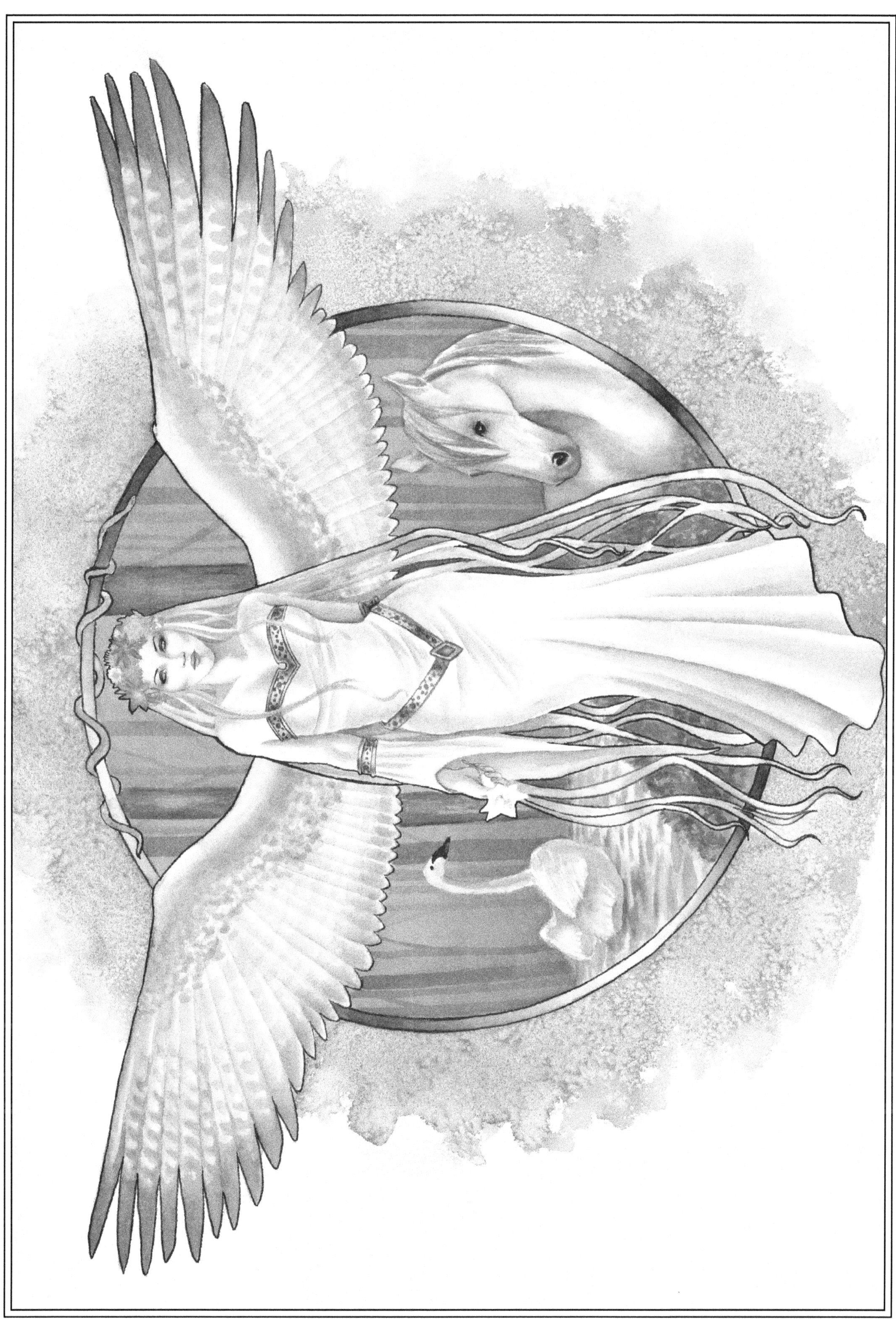

"Warm my Heart"

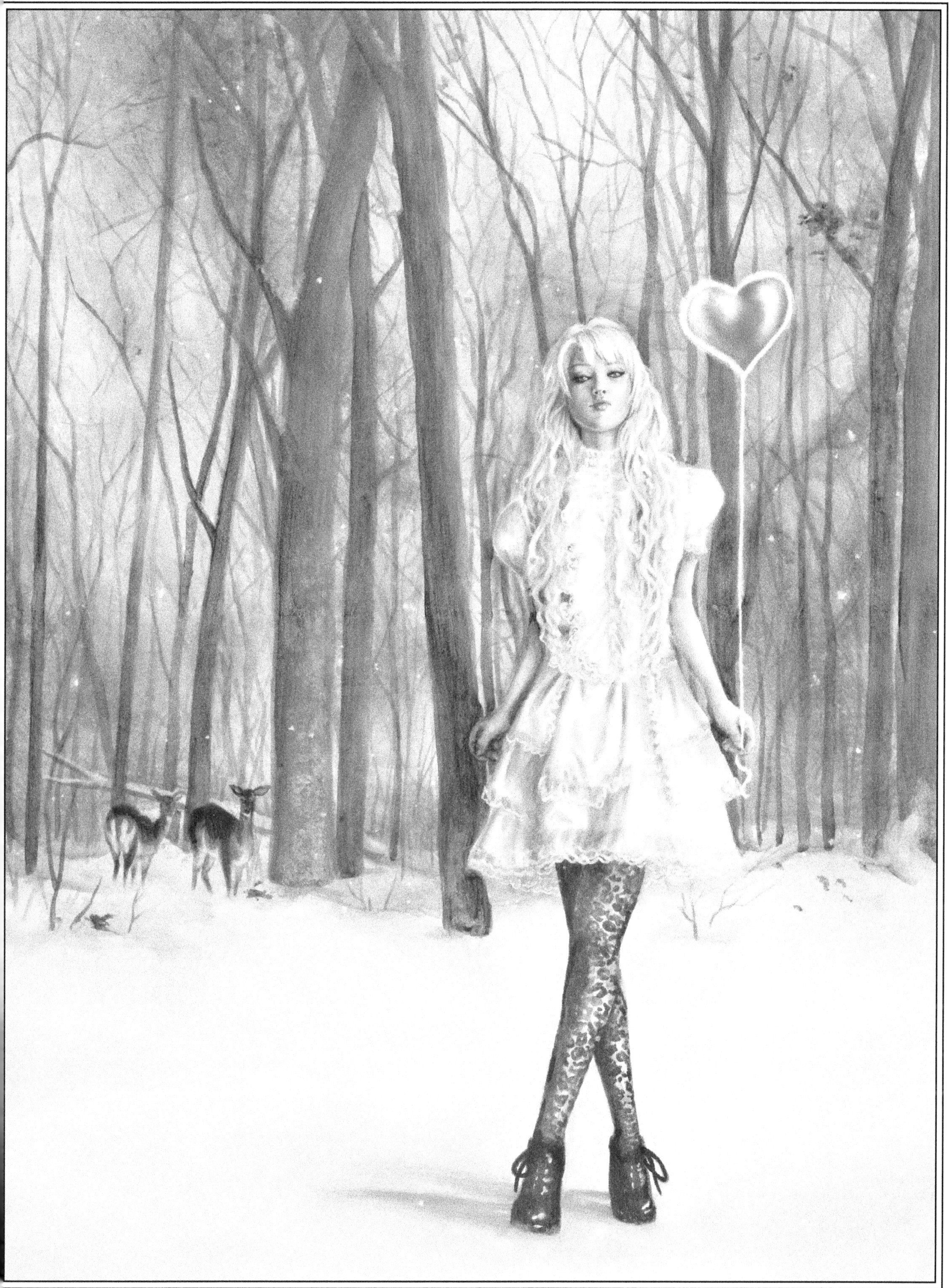

"Wandering Through The Woods"

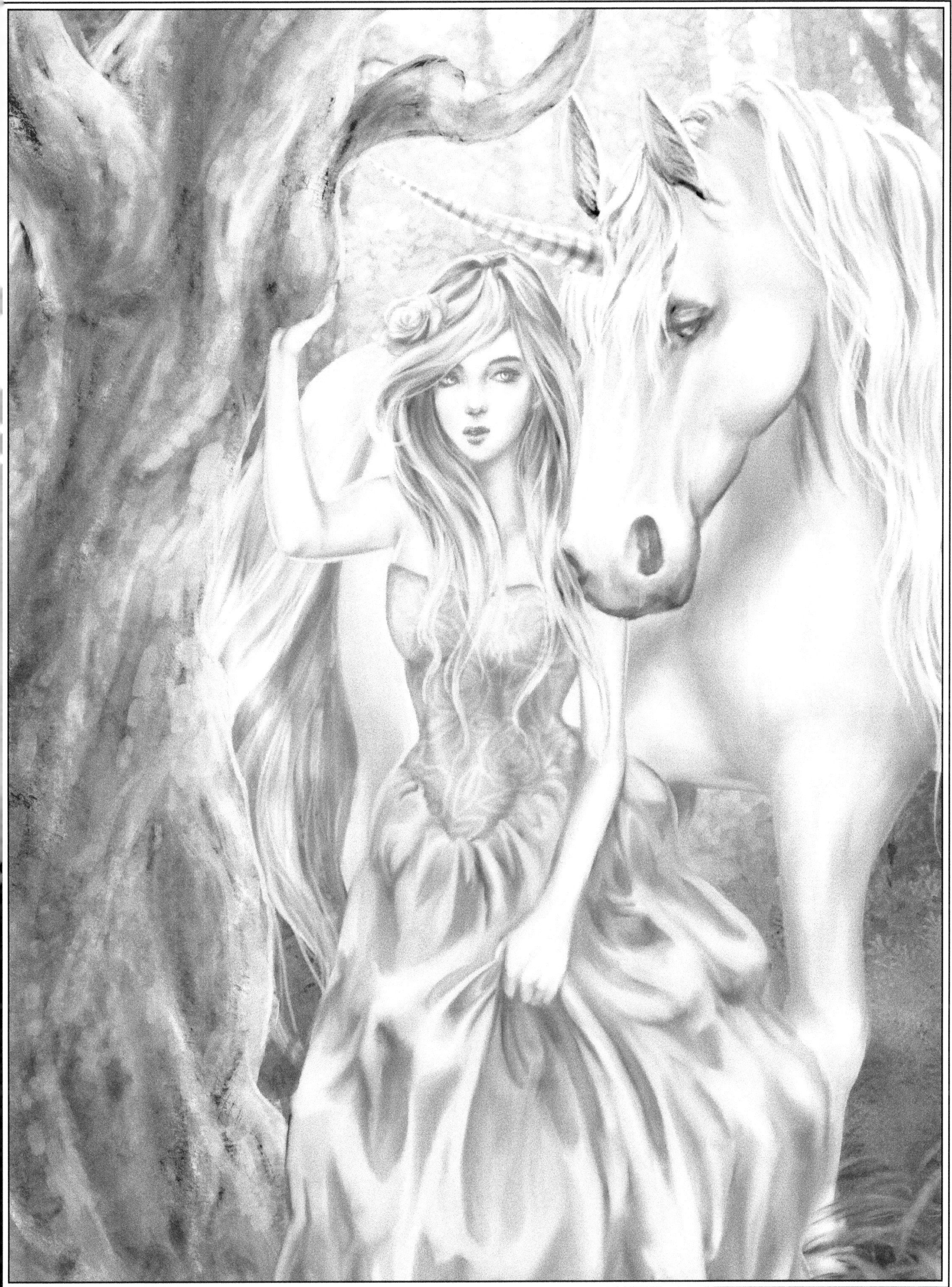

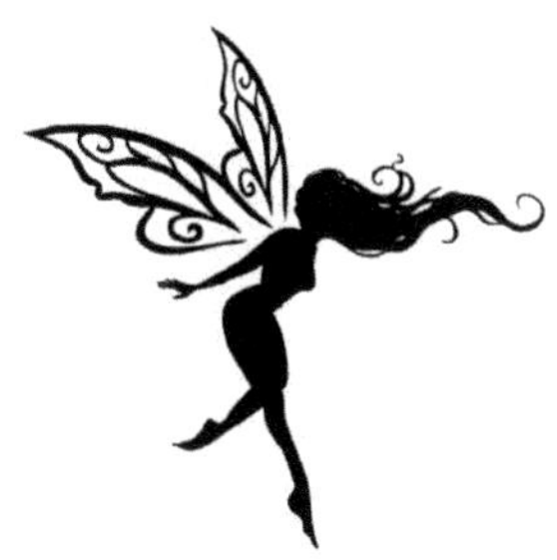

Second Set of Pages Begins Here

When designing my books I decided to print them with two copies of each design, because as an artist I know there are always so many possibilities! I also wanted to give everybody the chance of a do-over with every design in case of an oops (as an artist I know that happens too!). Try a different medium, or a different colour scheme. Or share the magic with a loved one. Because sharing your creativity and joy of color is the best magic of all. ~ *Selina*

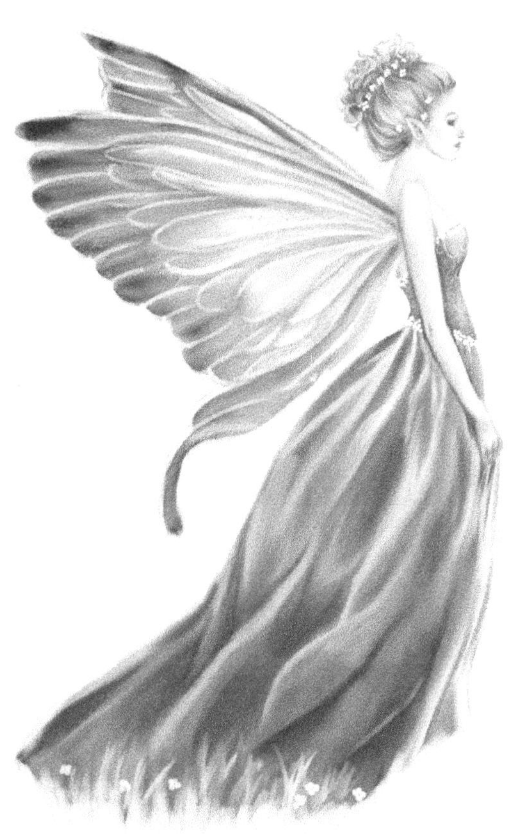

"Autumn Slumber"

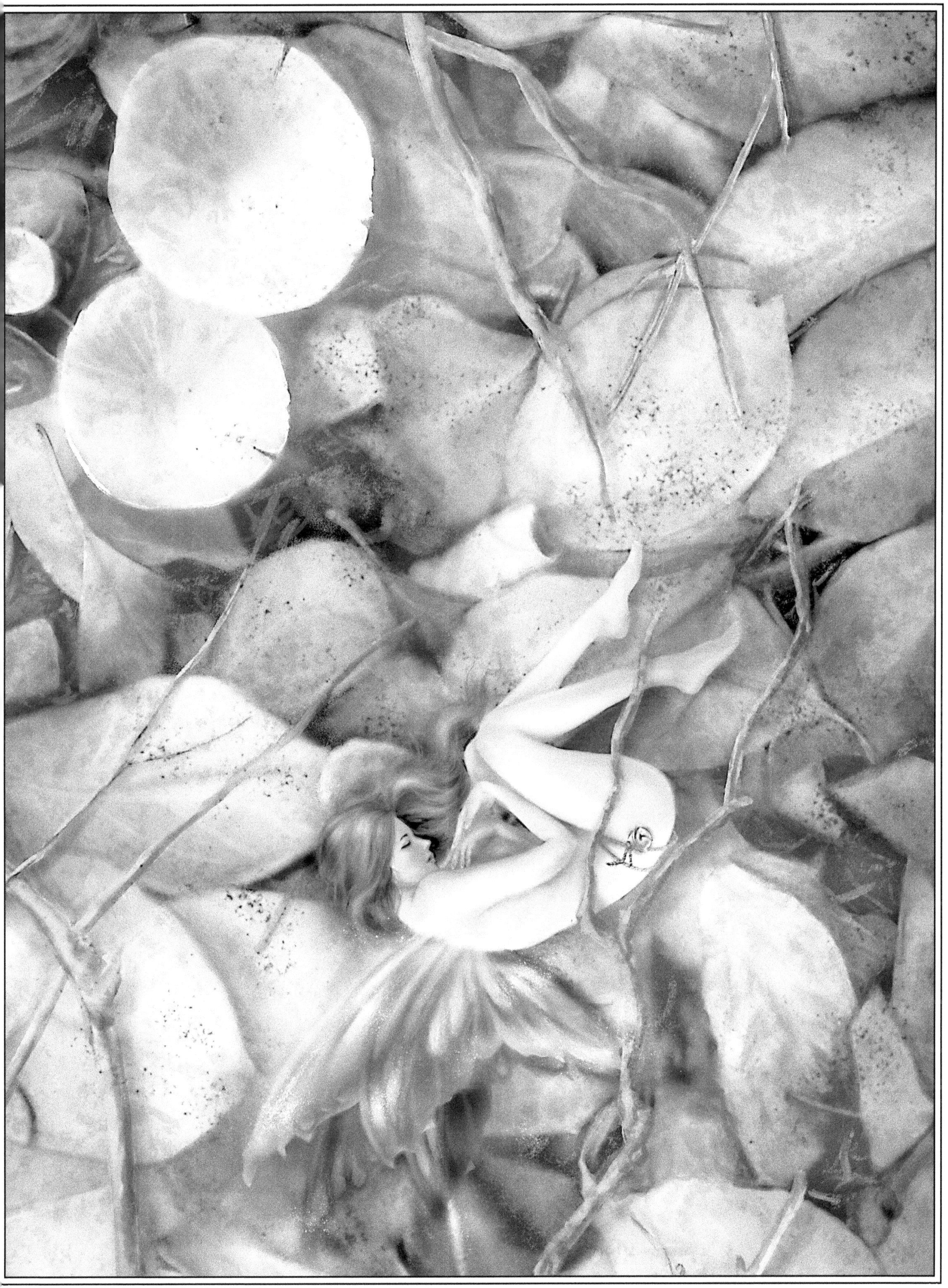

"To Meet a Dragon"

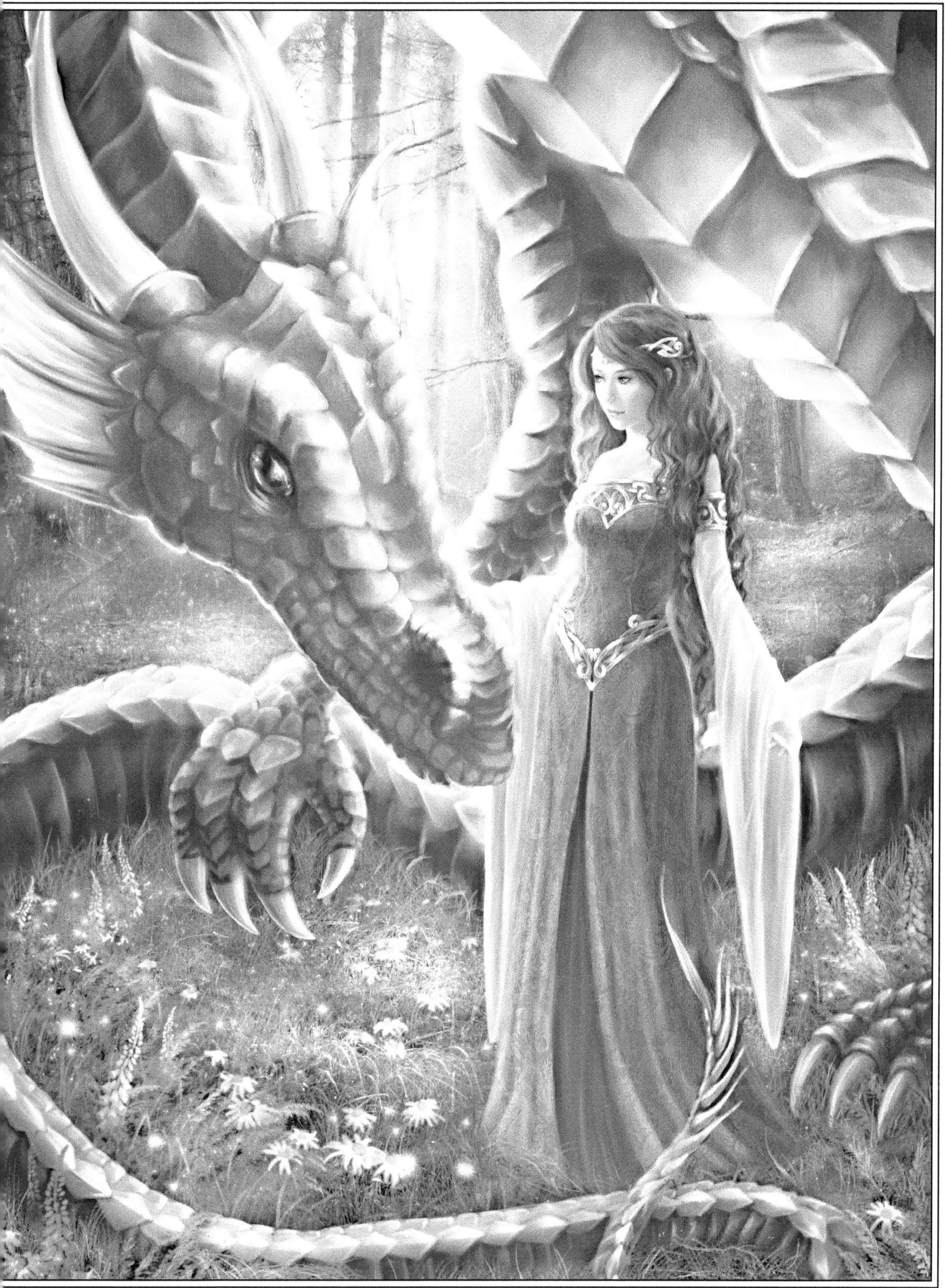

“Hatchling”

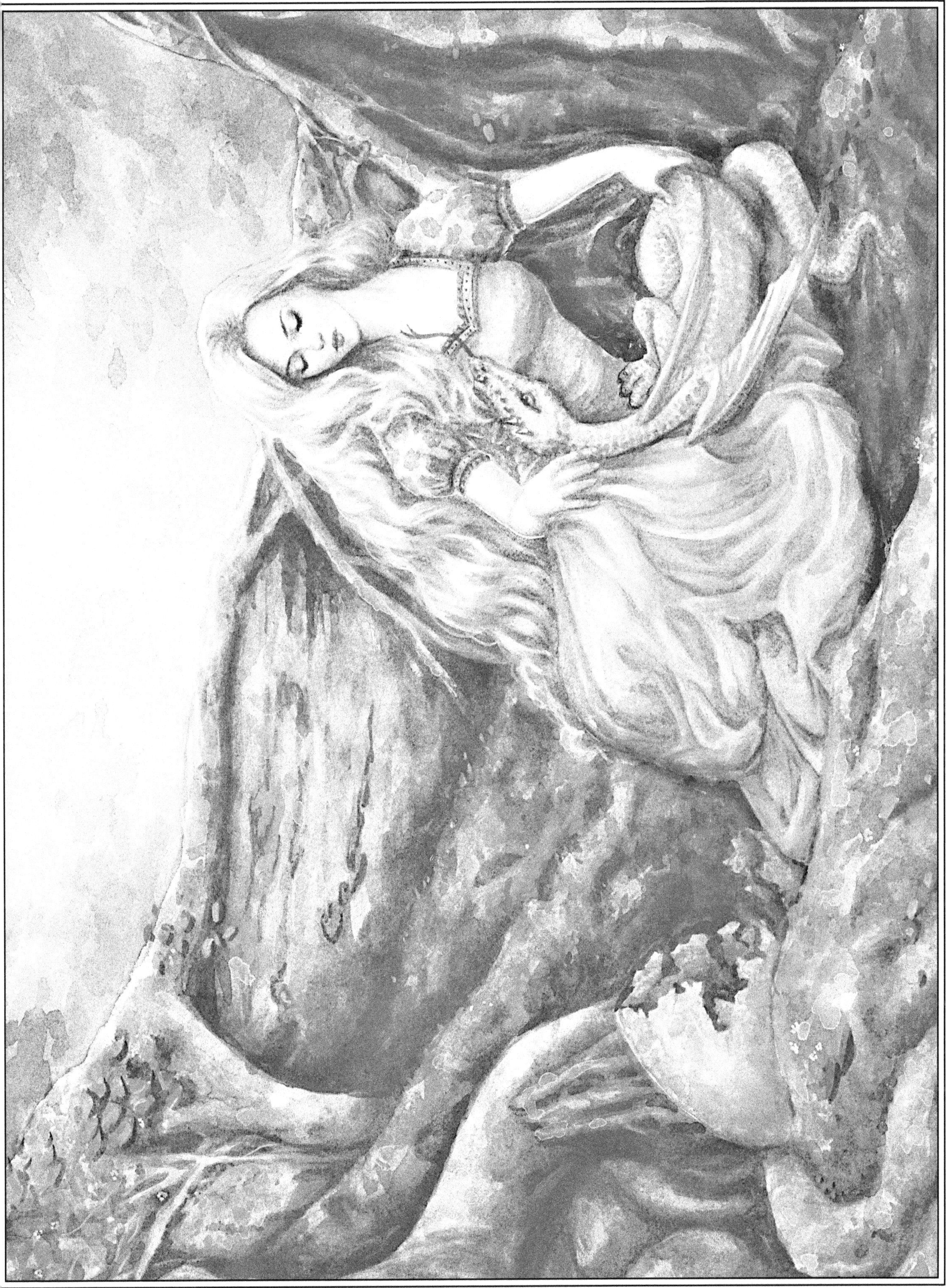

"Twilight Stroll"

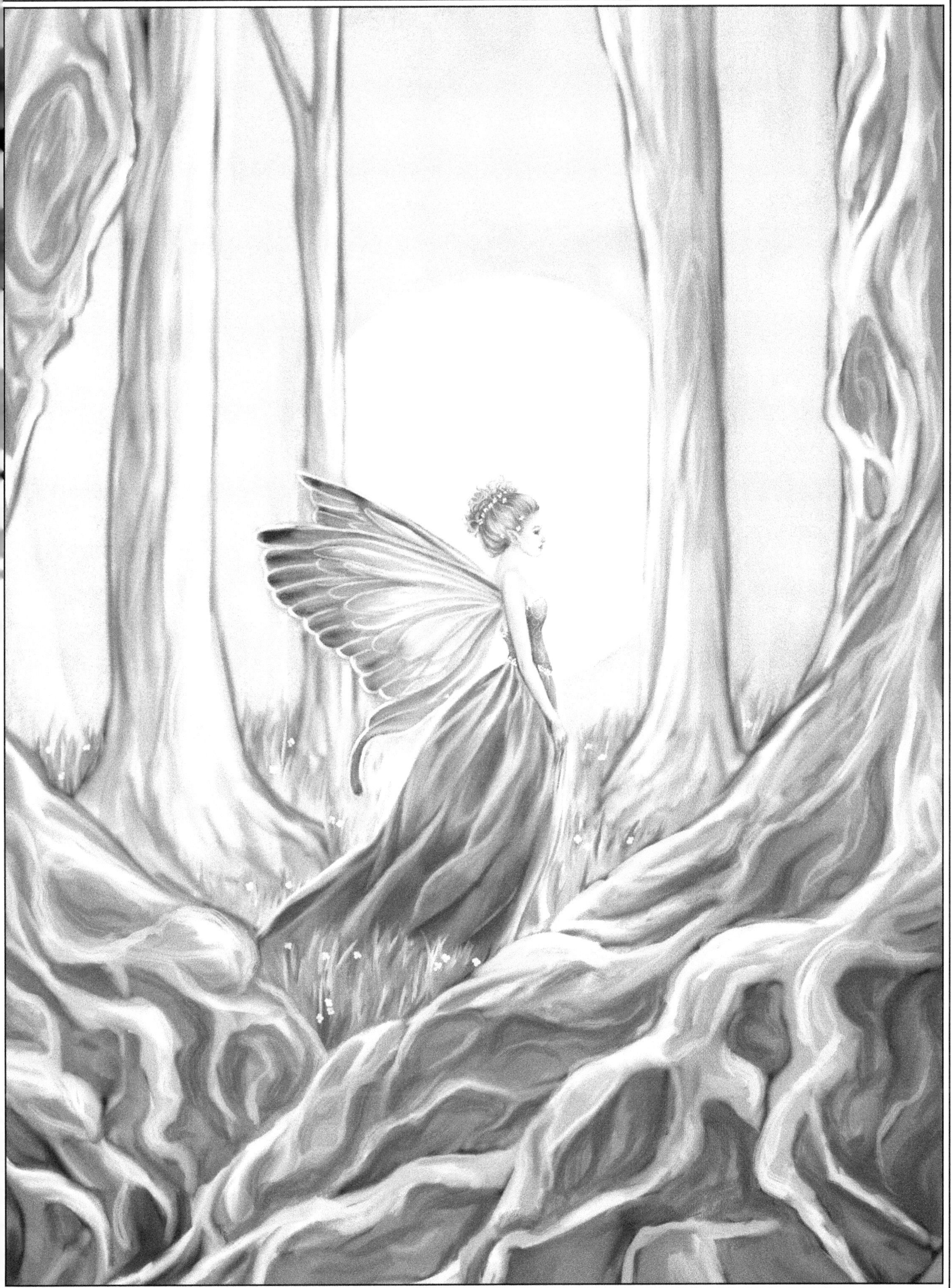

"Along the Forest Path"

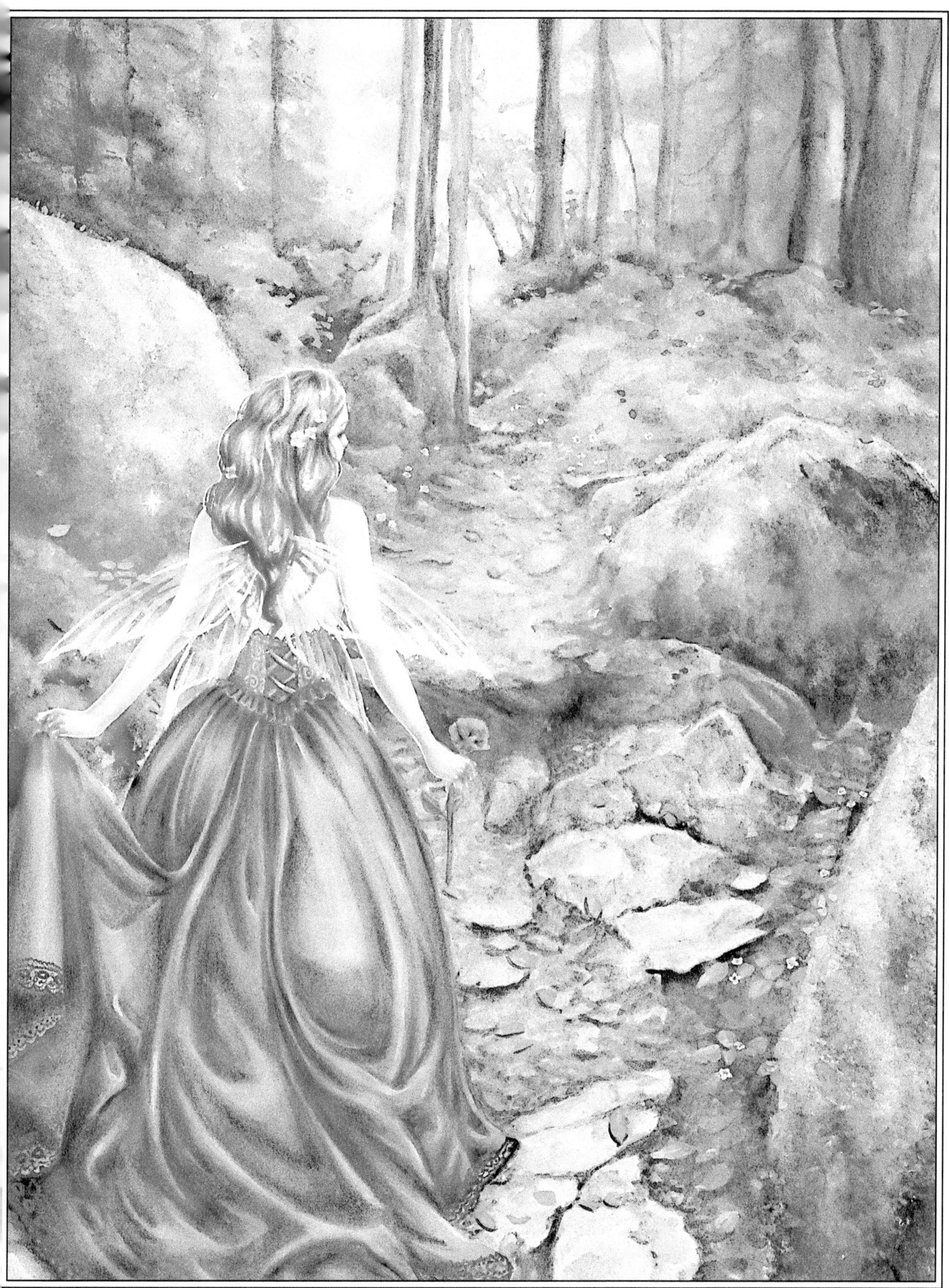

"Blodeuwedd in Bloom"

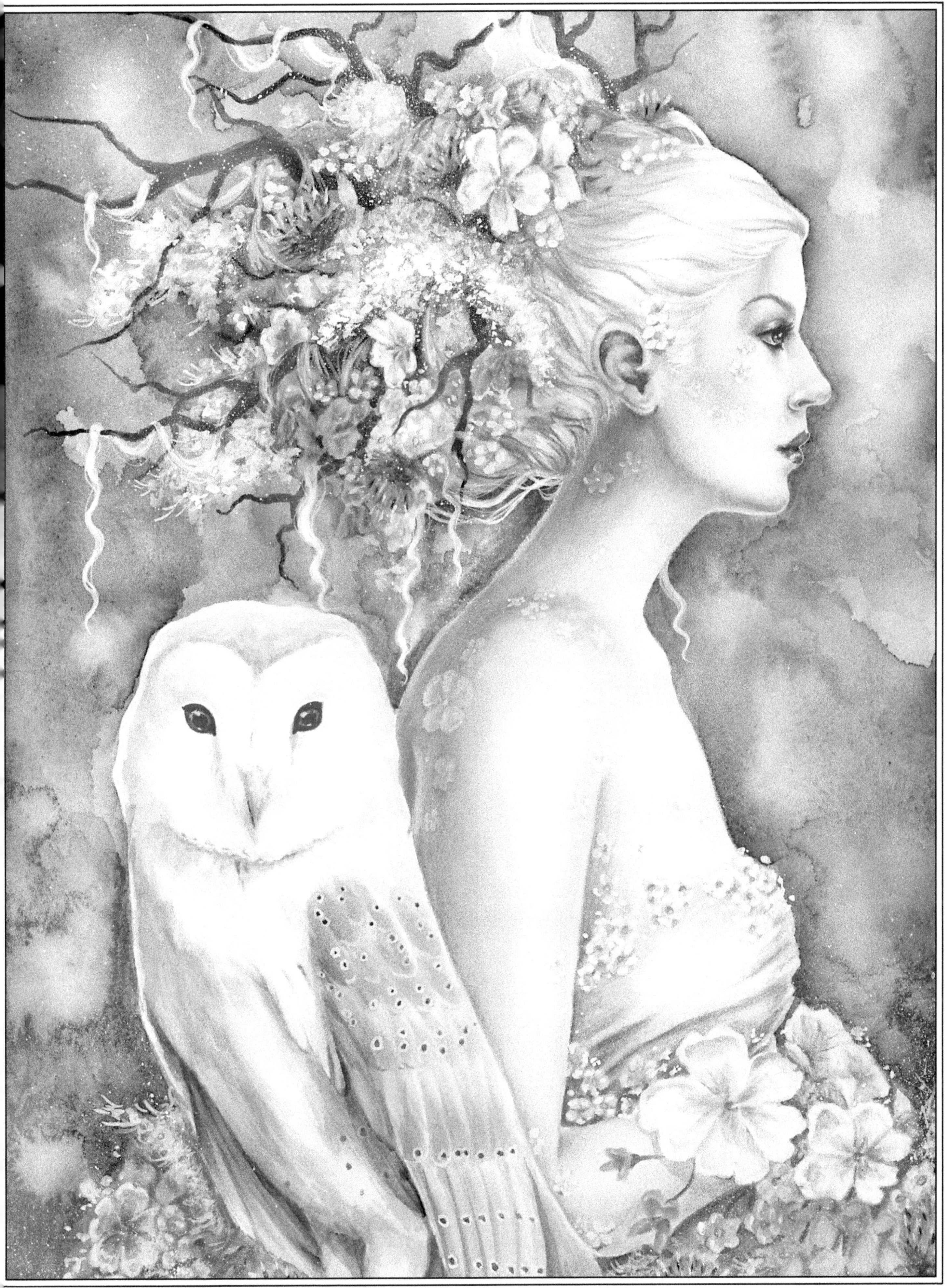

"Dance of the Graces"

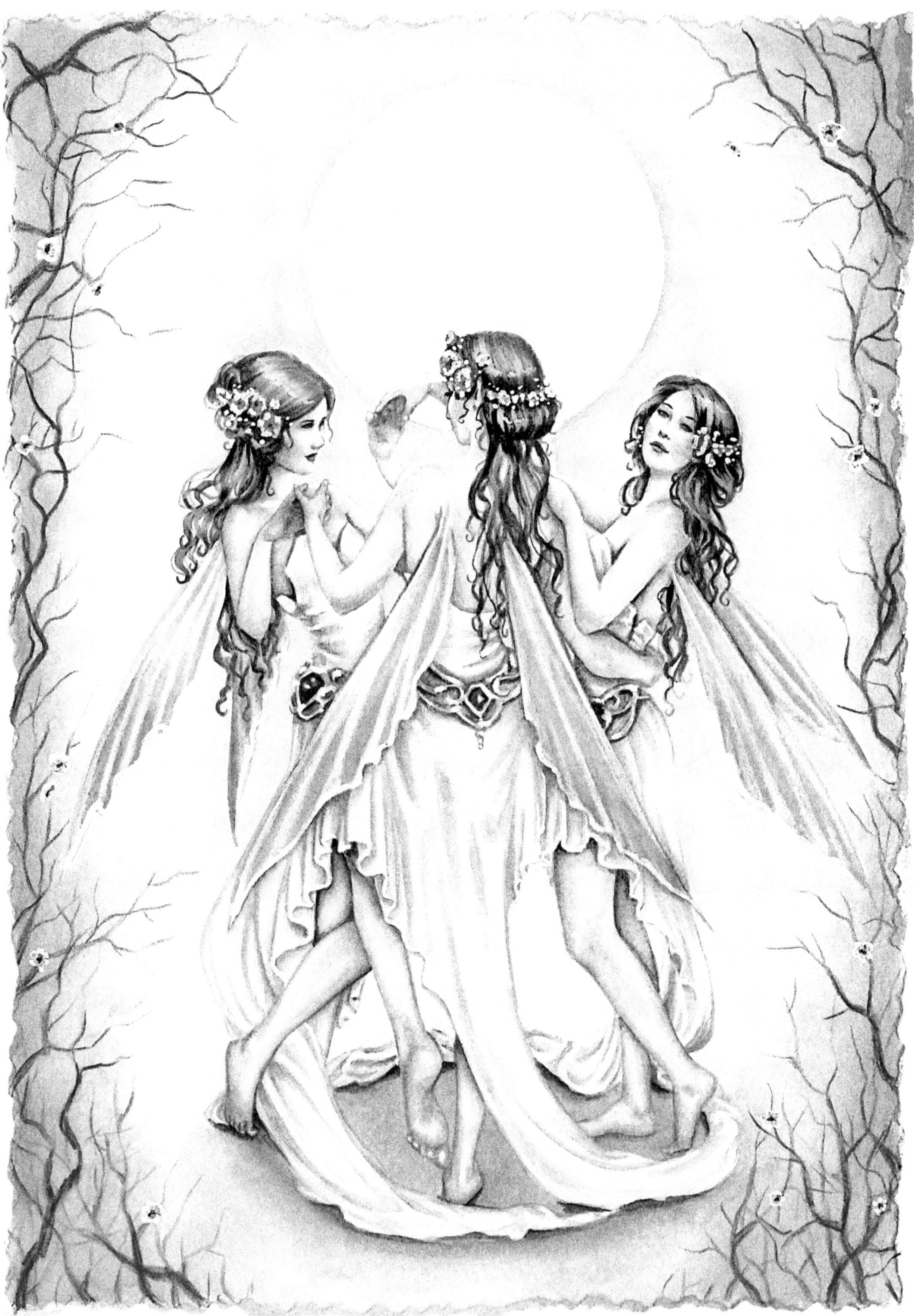

"Earth, Life, Magic"

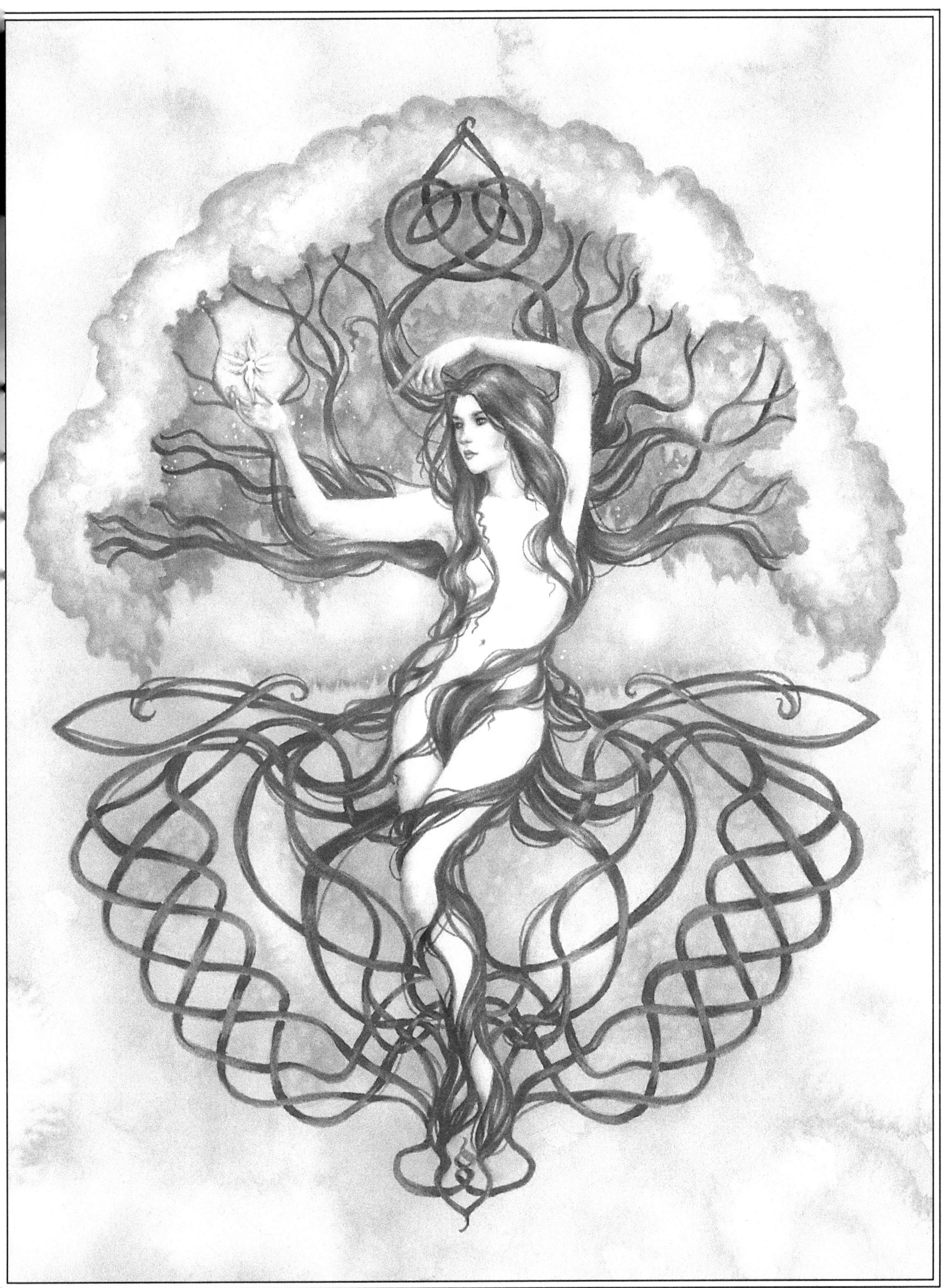

"Moonlit Kiss"

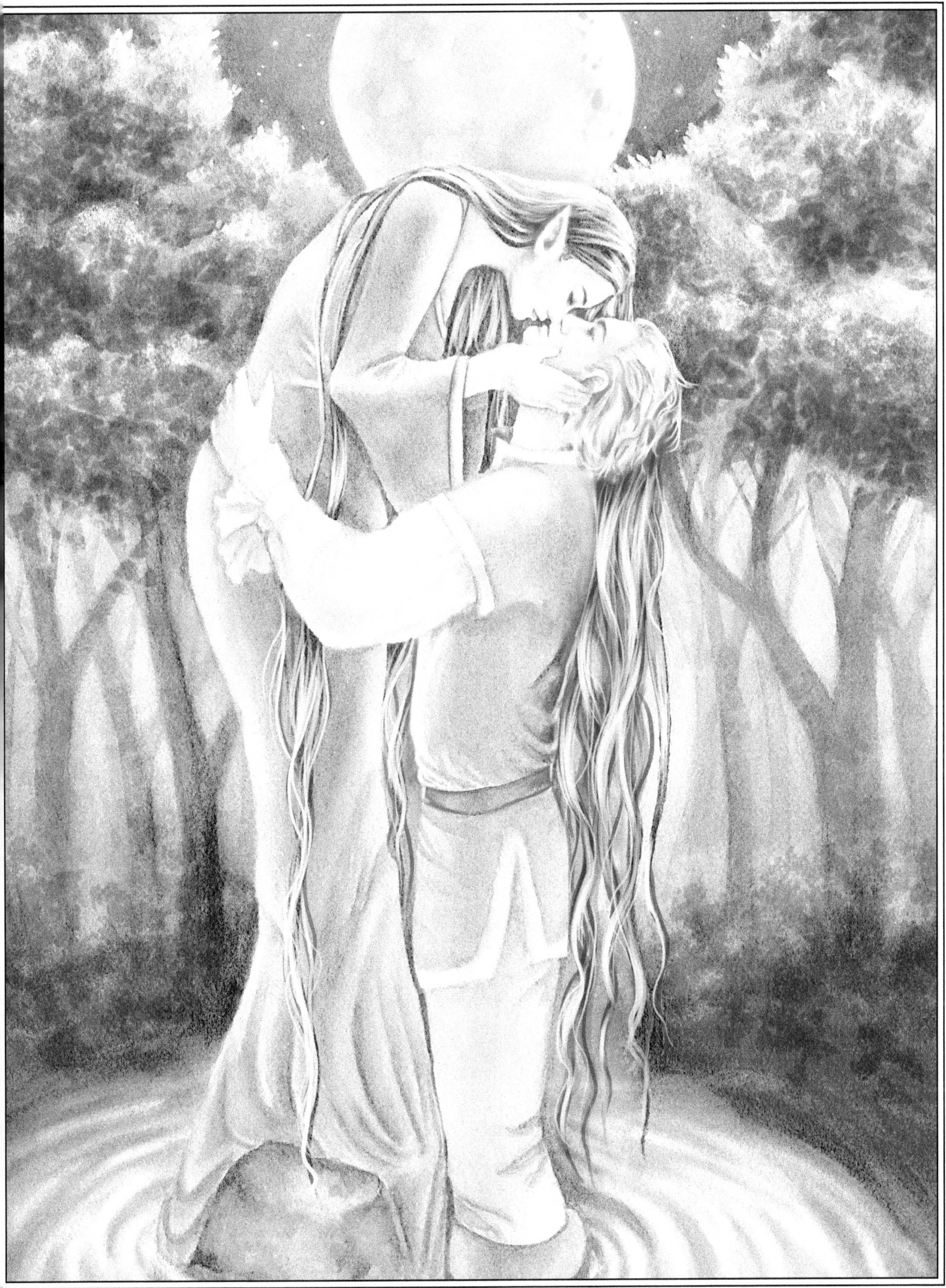

"Fairy Wishing Well"

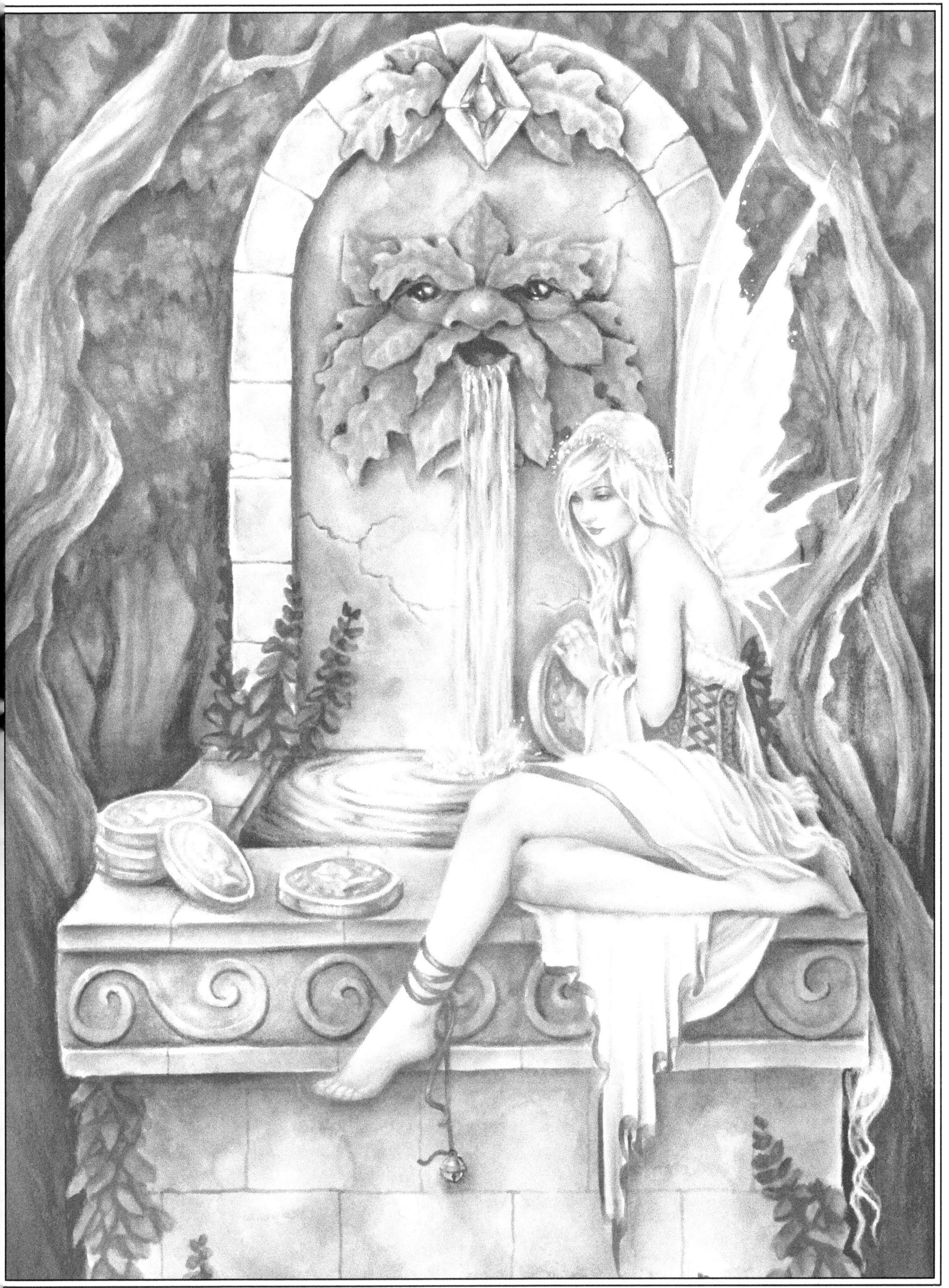

“Glimpse”

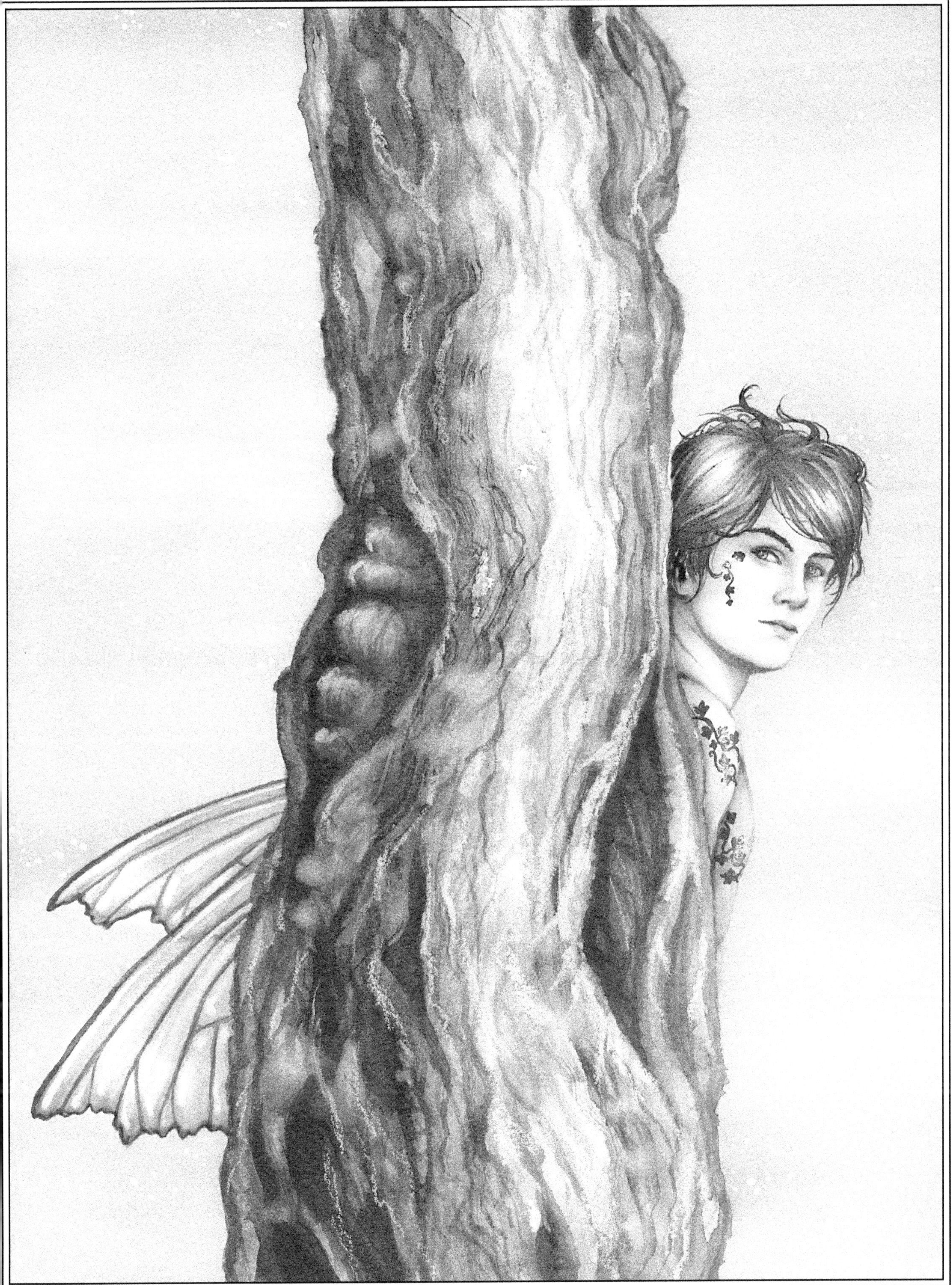

"Hide and Seek"

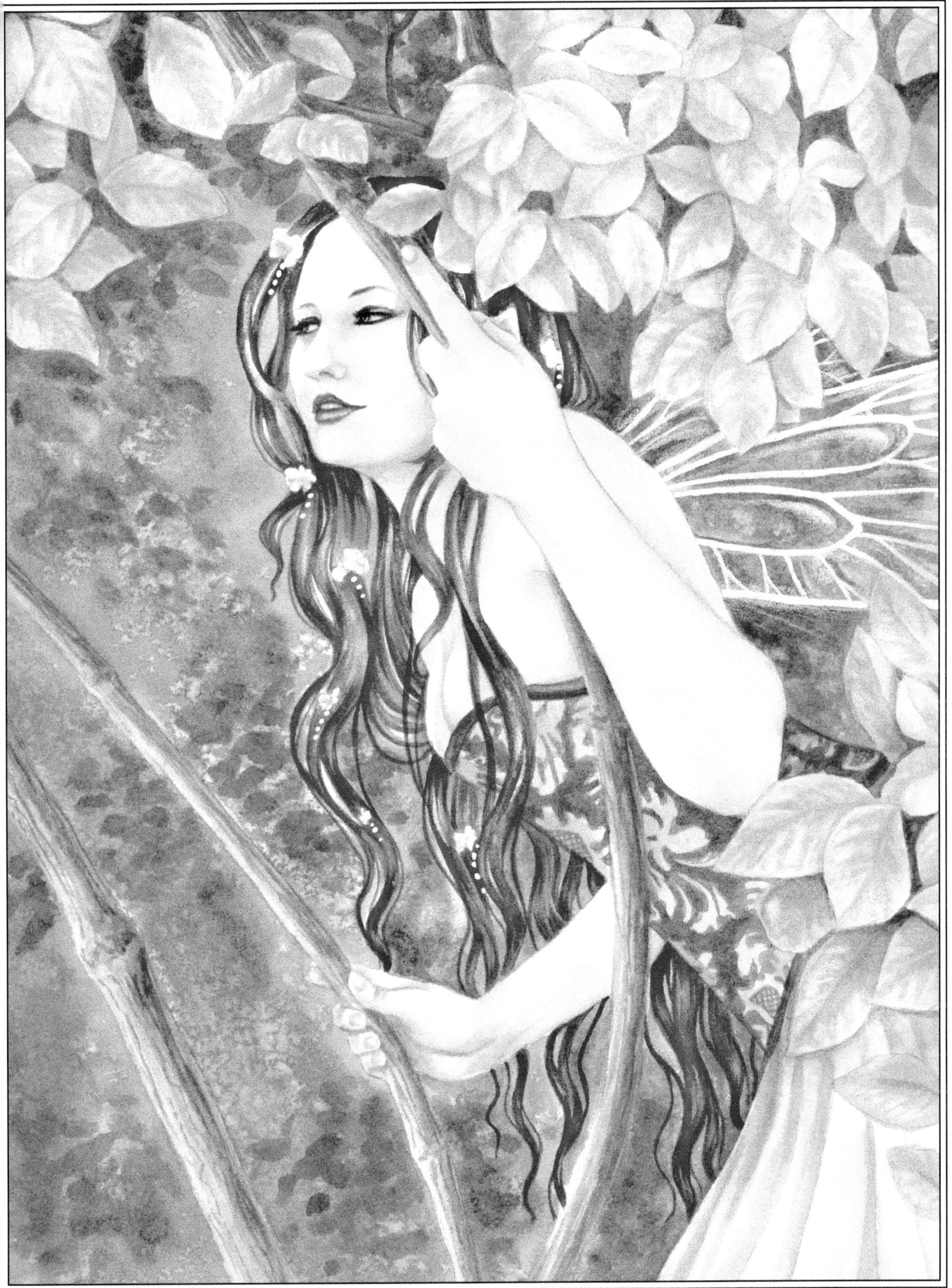

“Into the Woods”

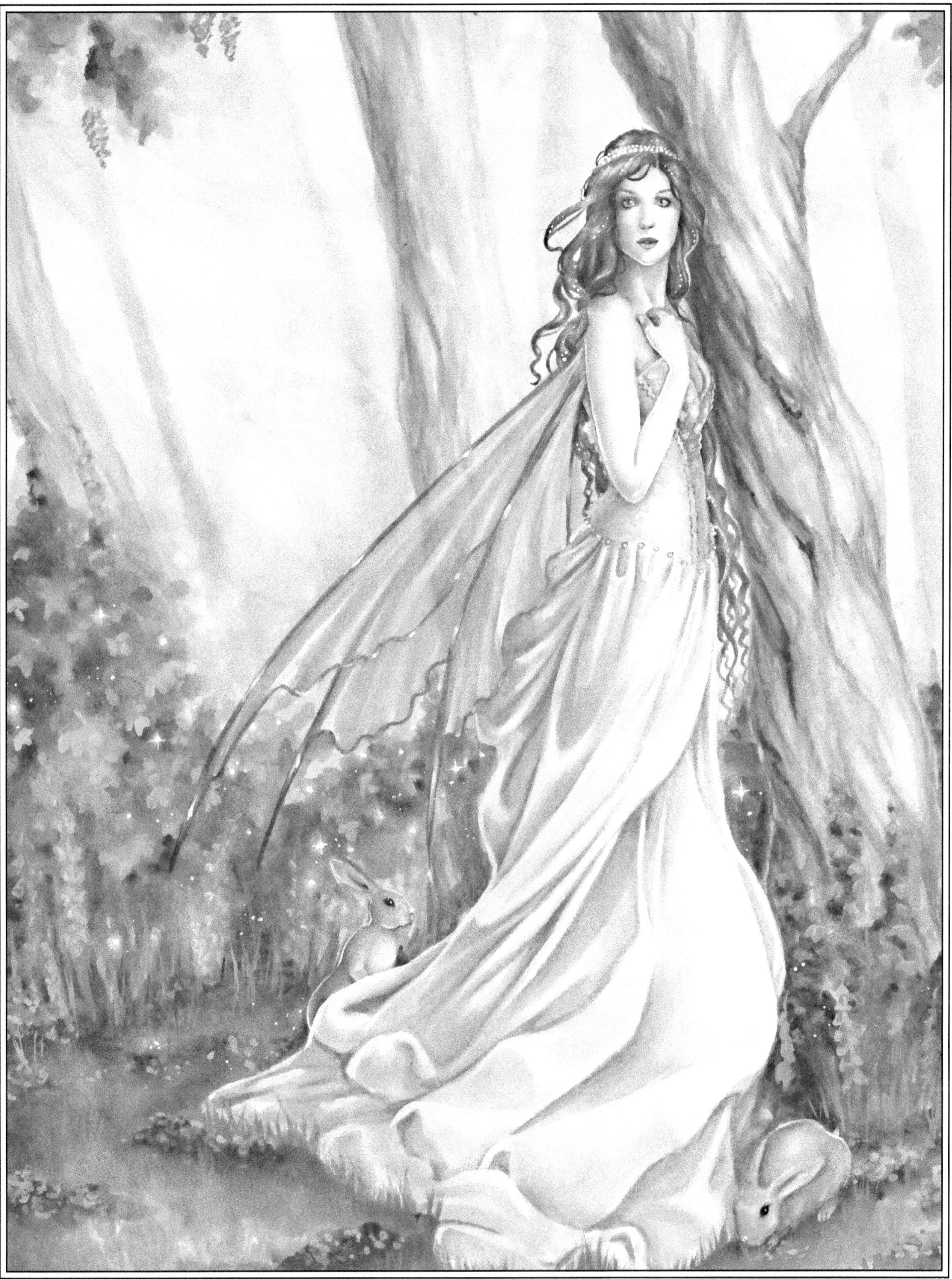

“Kindred”

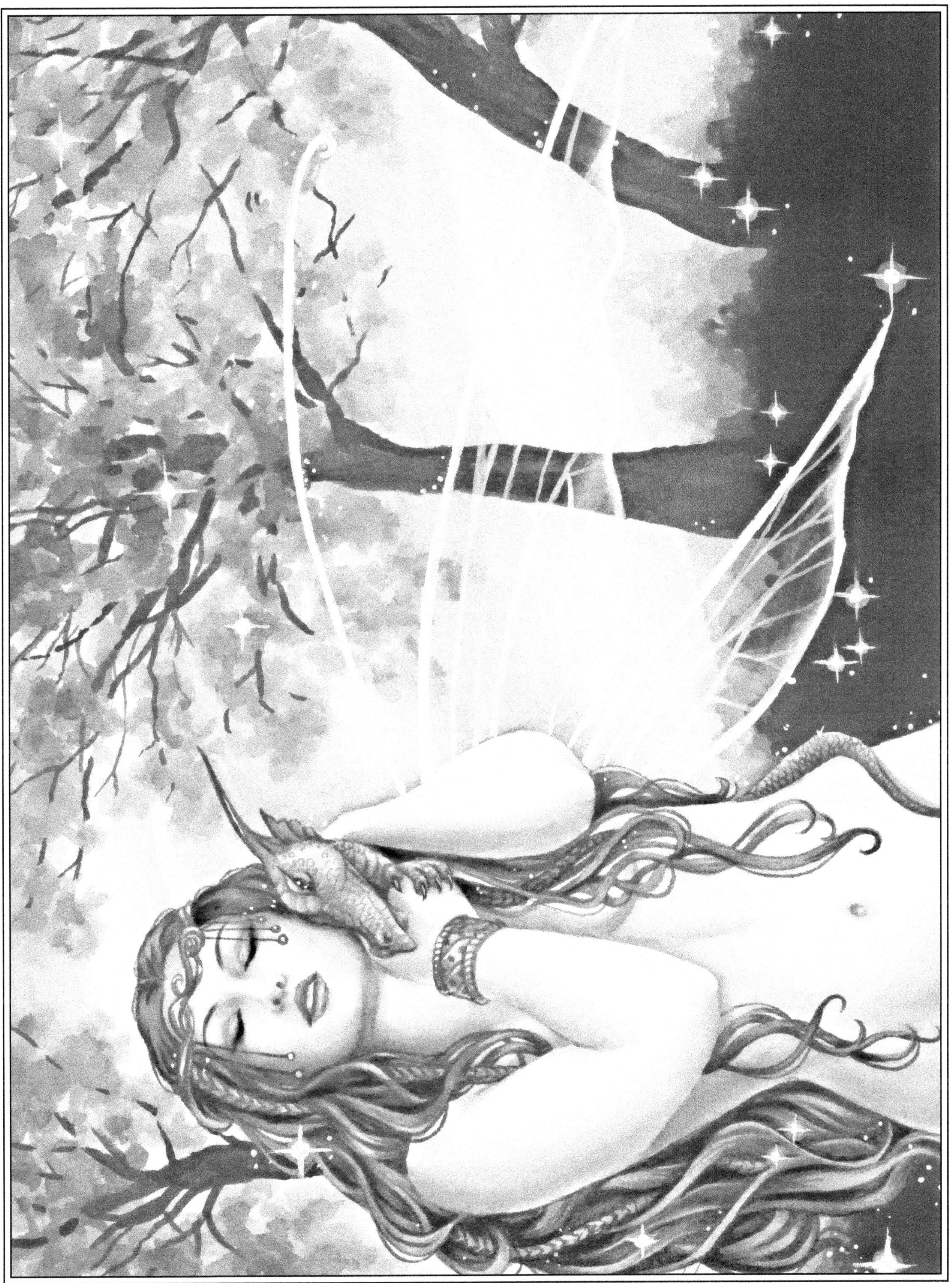

"Lilac Magic"

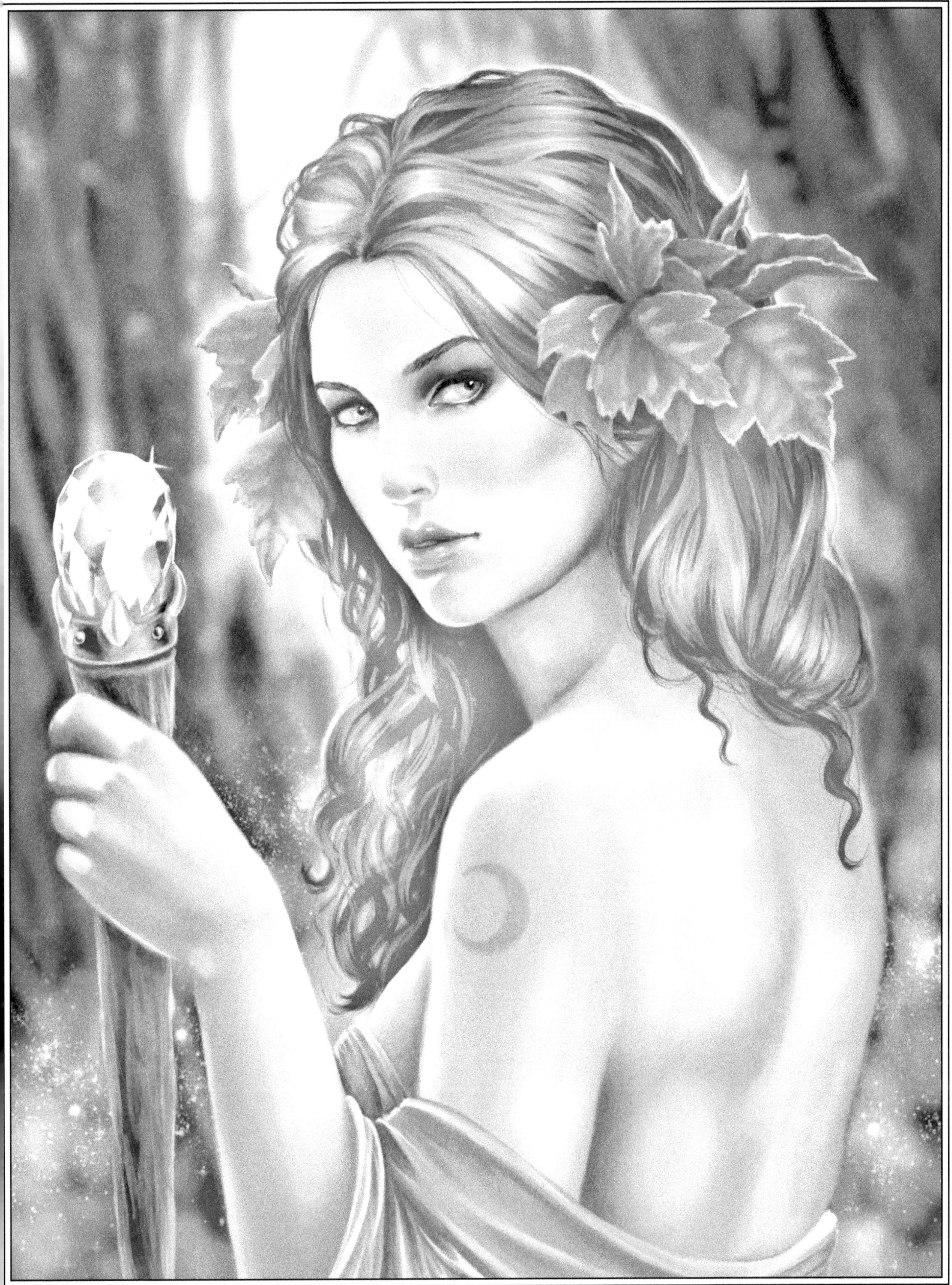

"Magic and Moonlight"

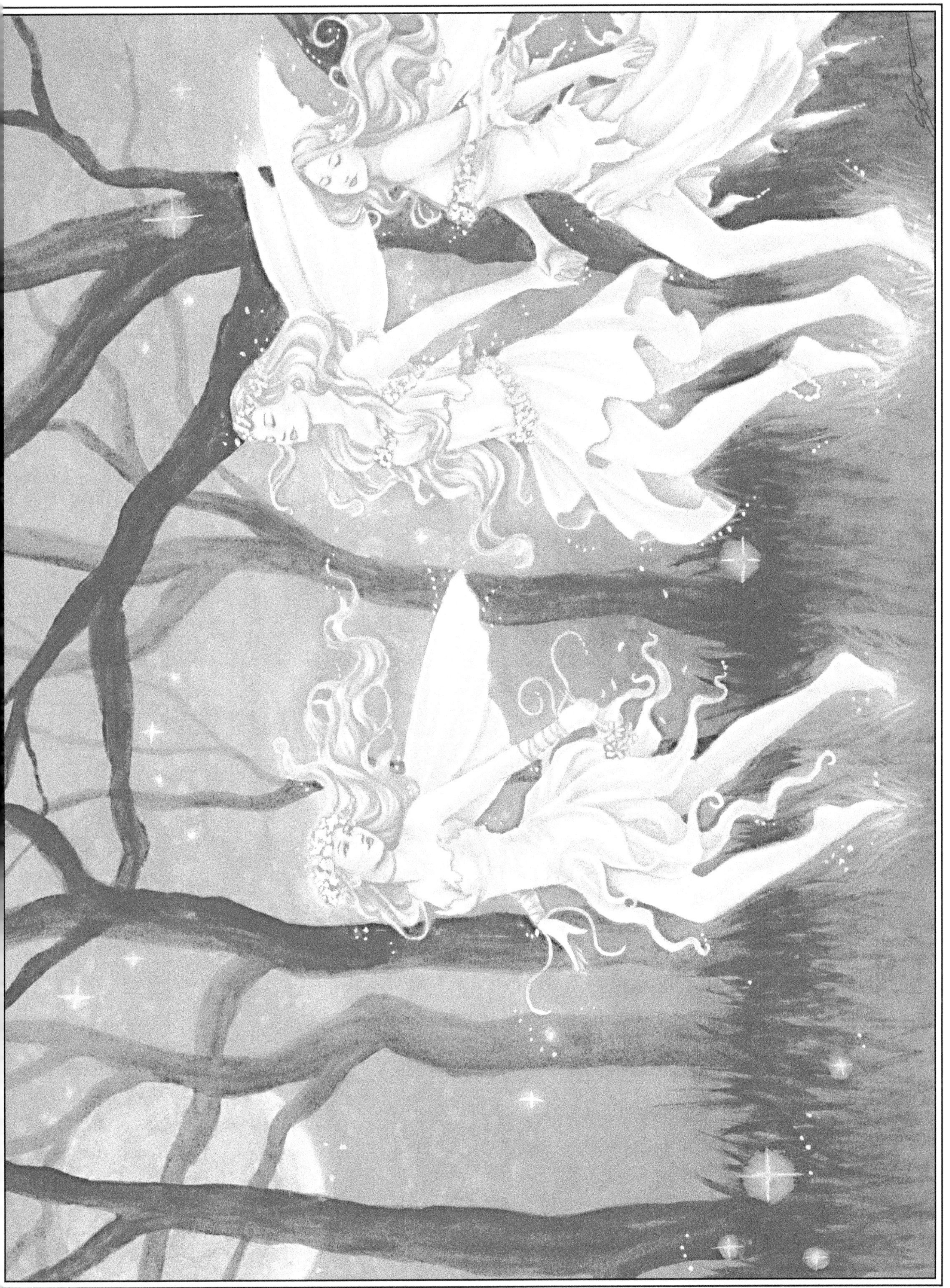

"Morgana's Secret"

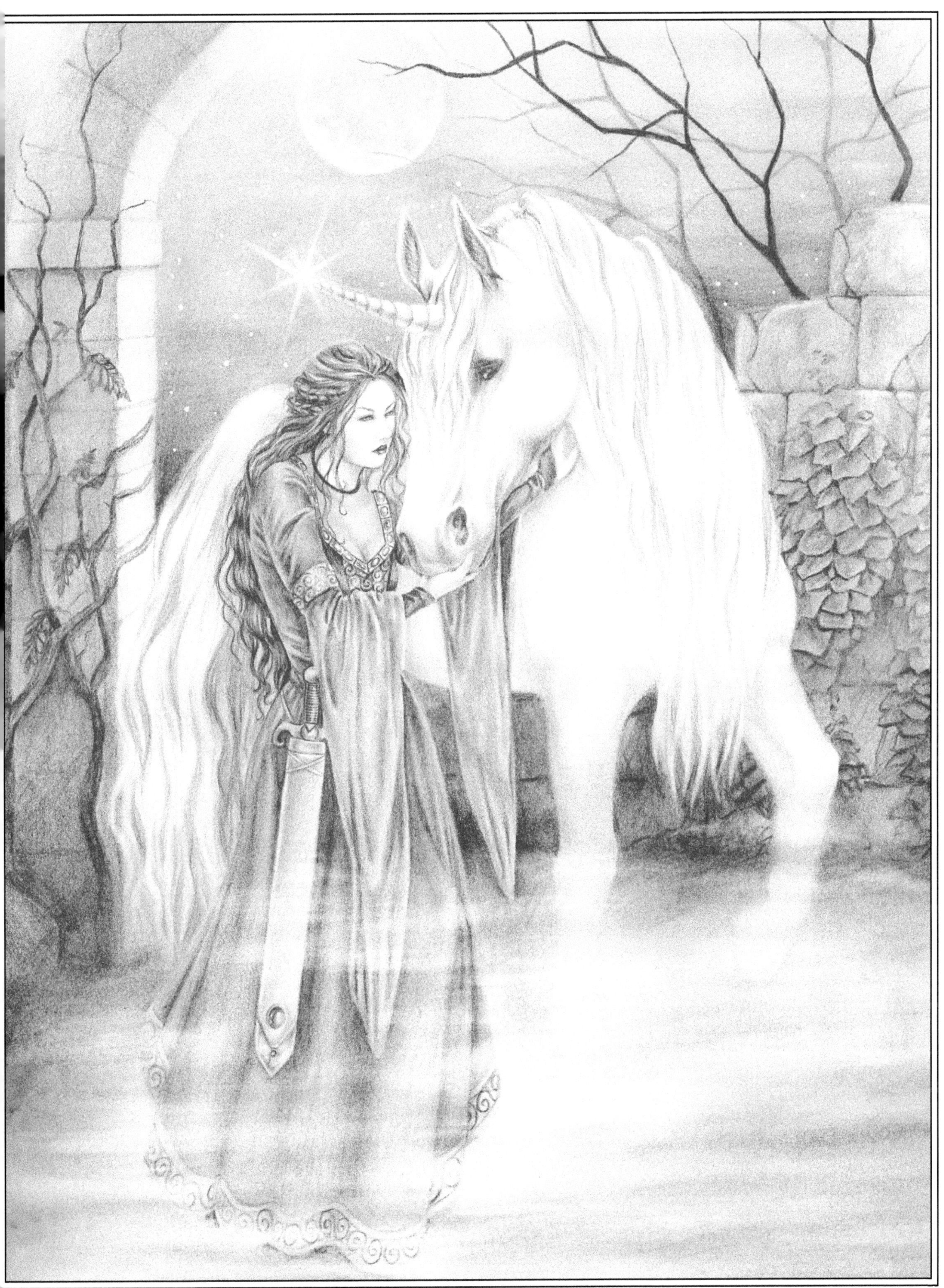

“Ravenkin”

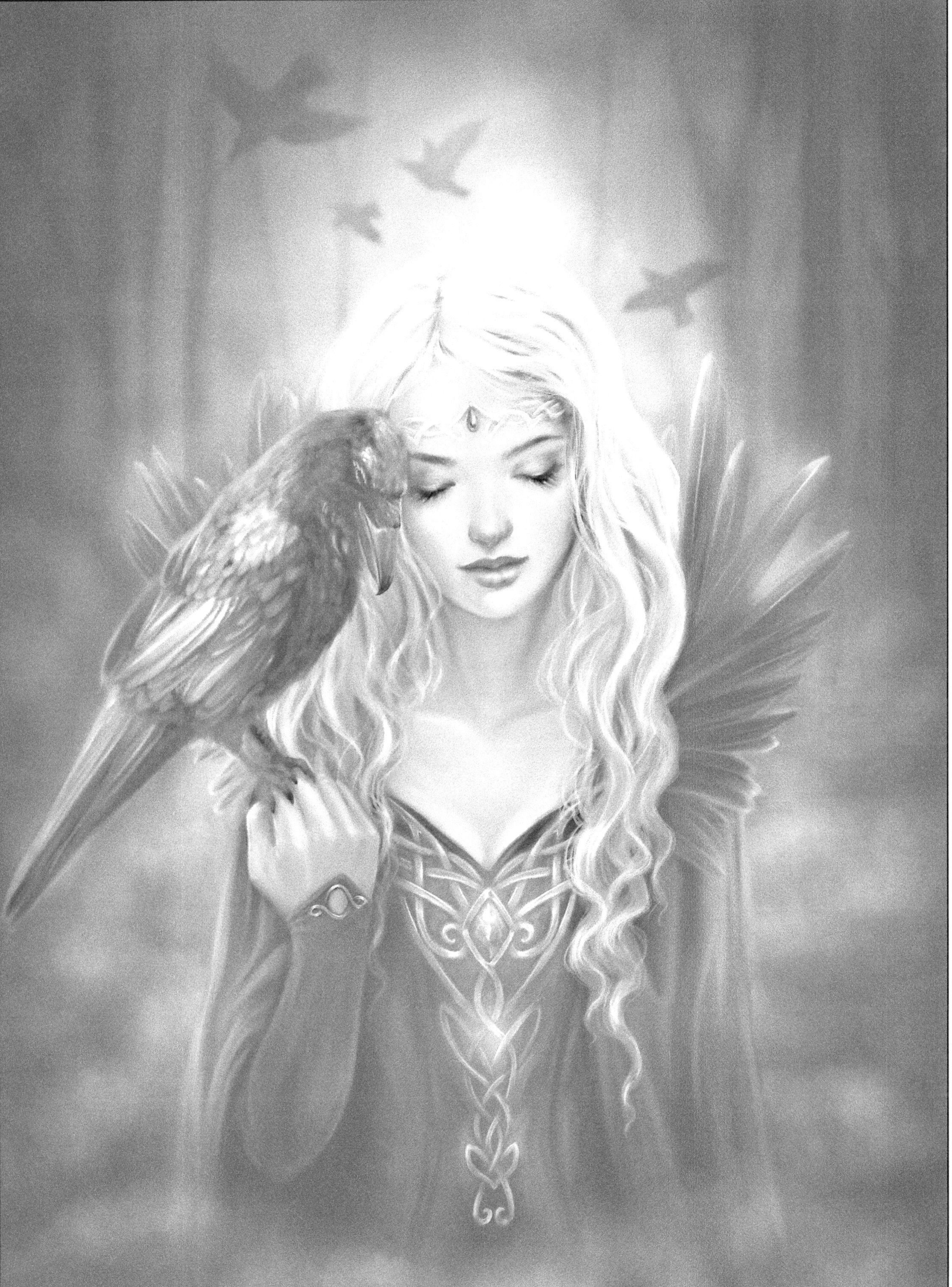

“Rockabye”

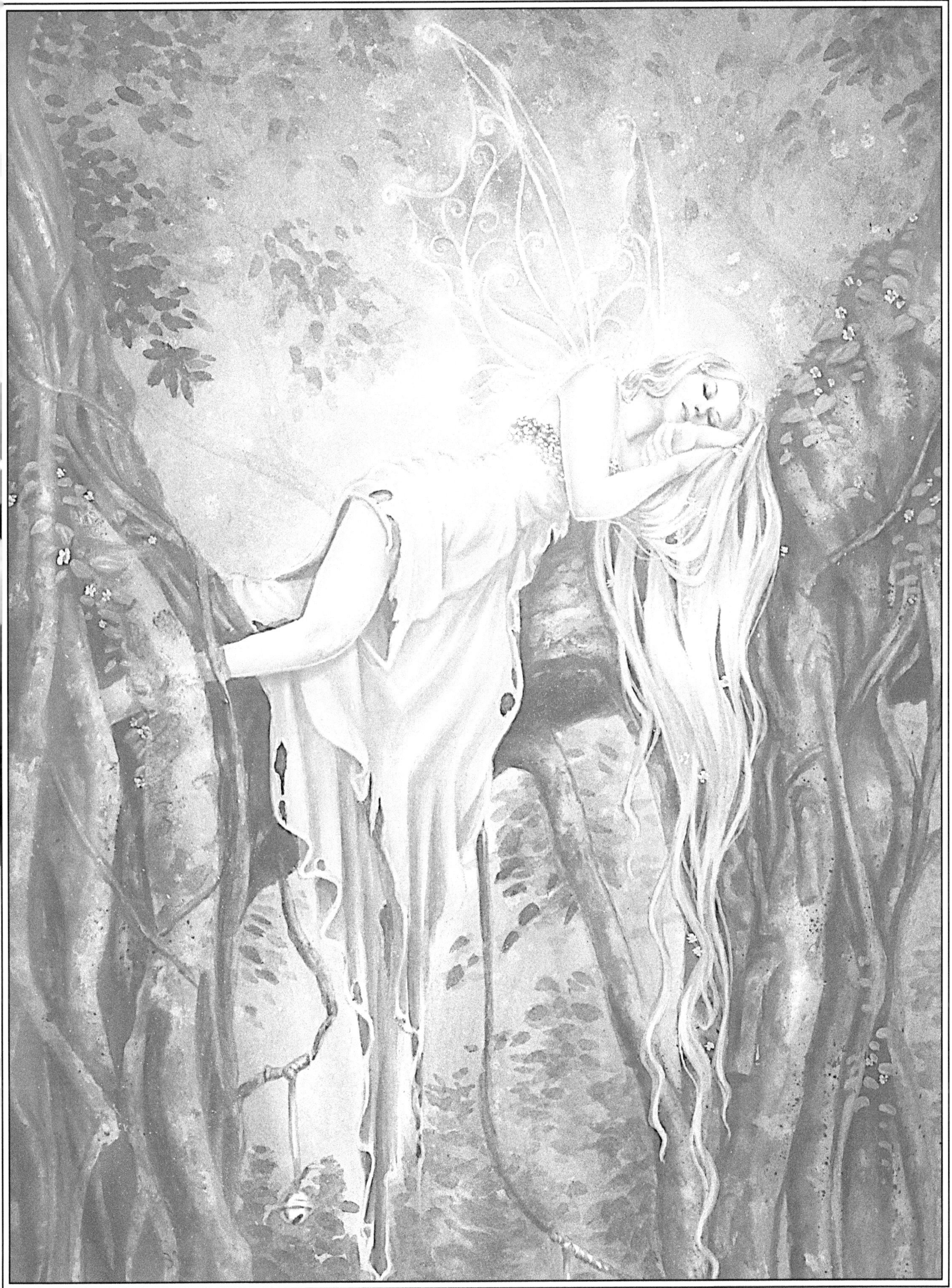

"Secret Doorway"

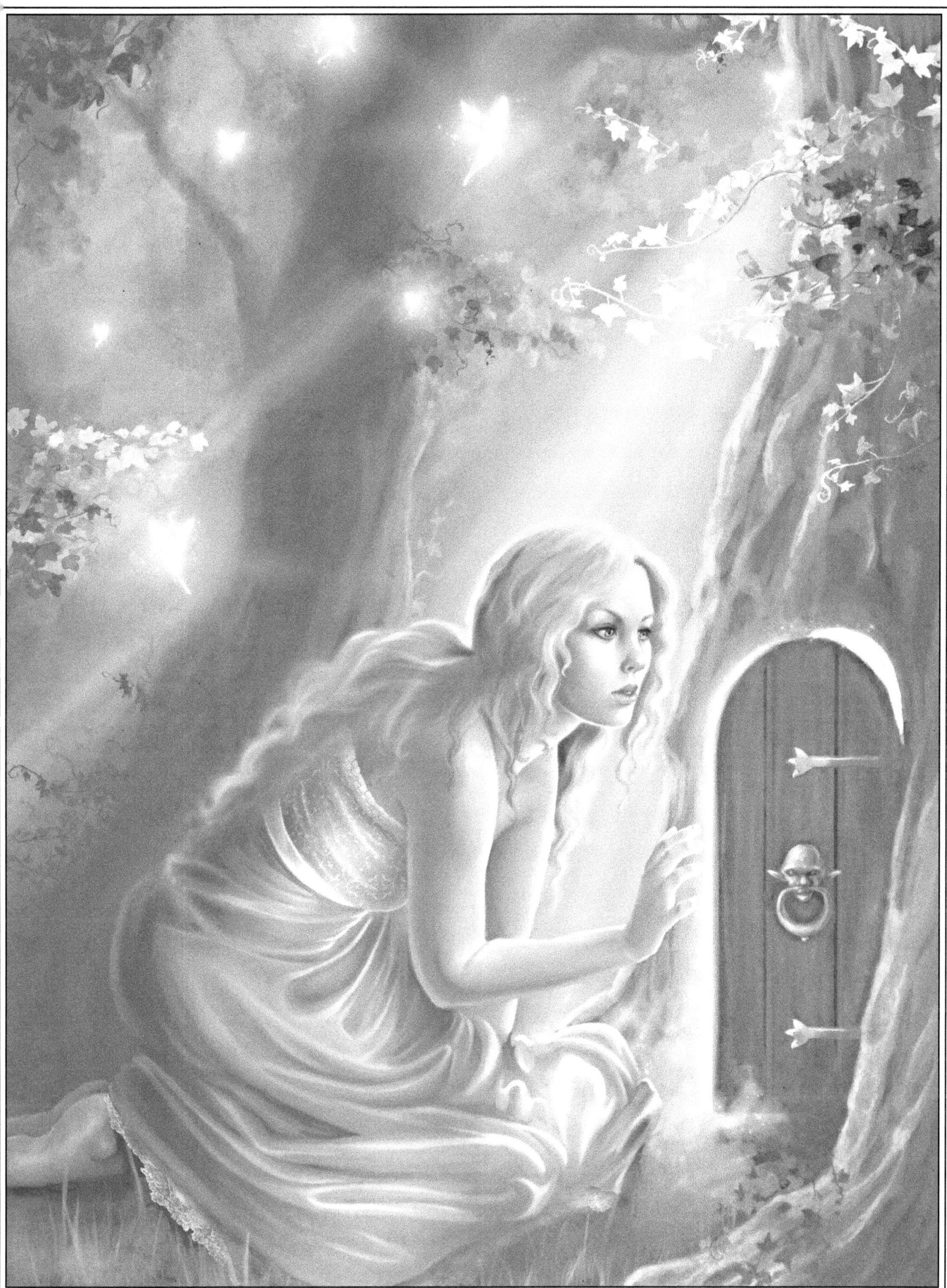

"Sleepy Spring"

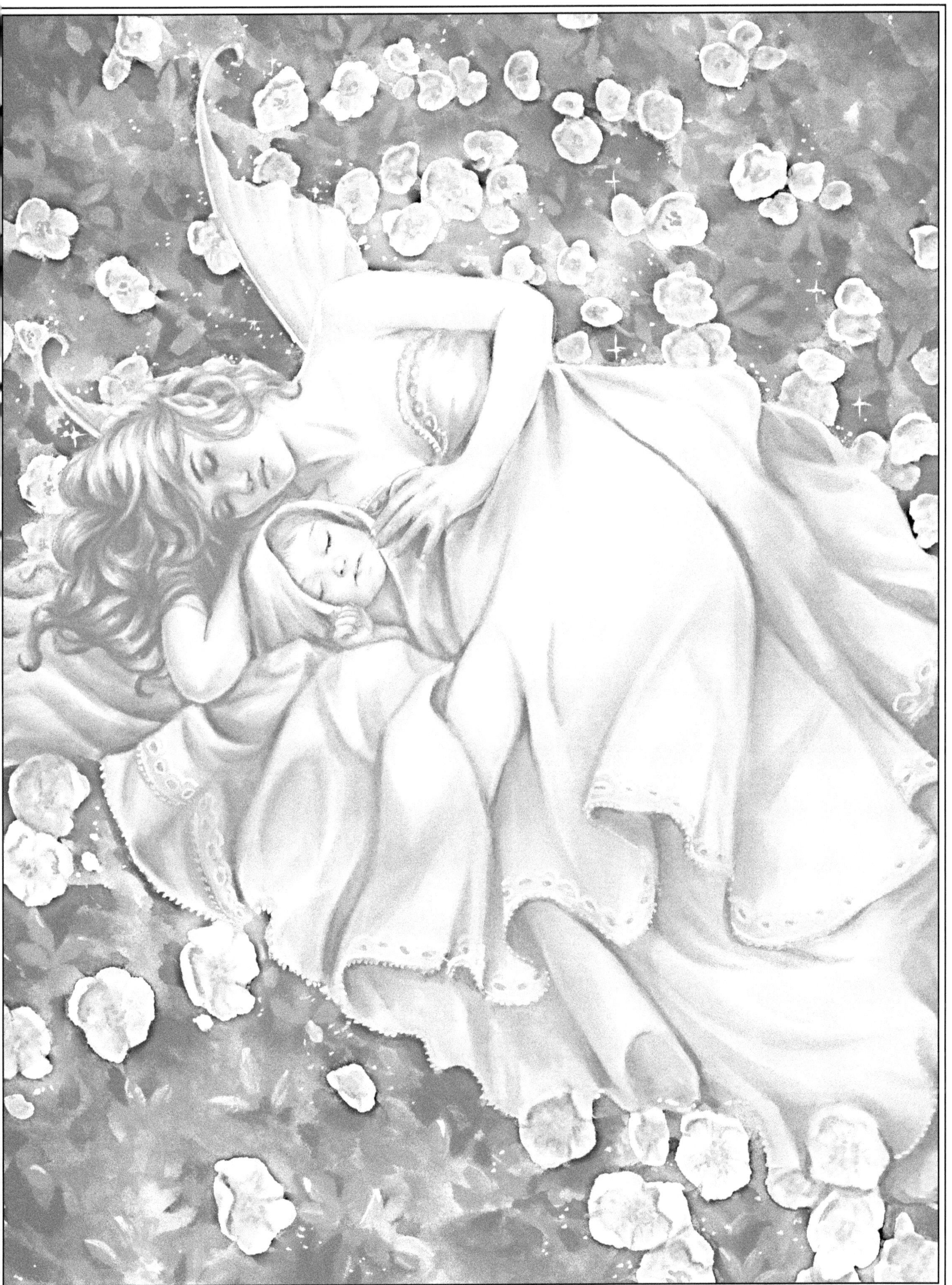

"Nature's Magic"

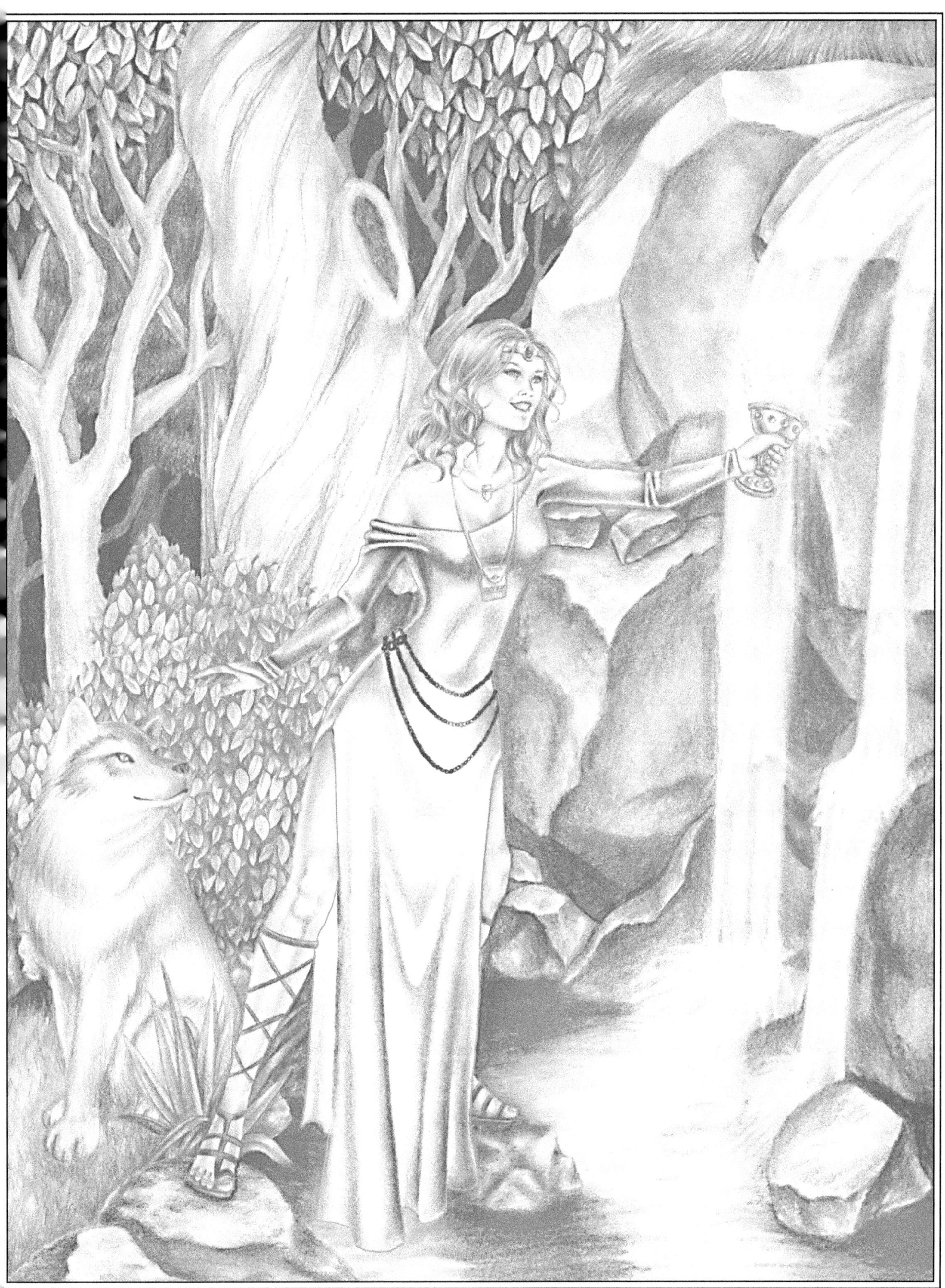

“Vila - Nature’s Angel”

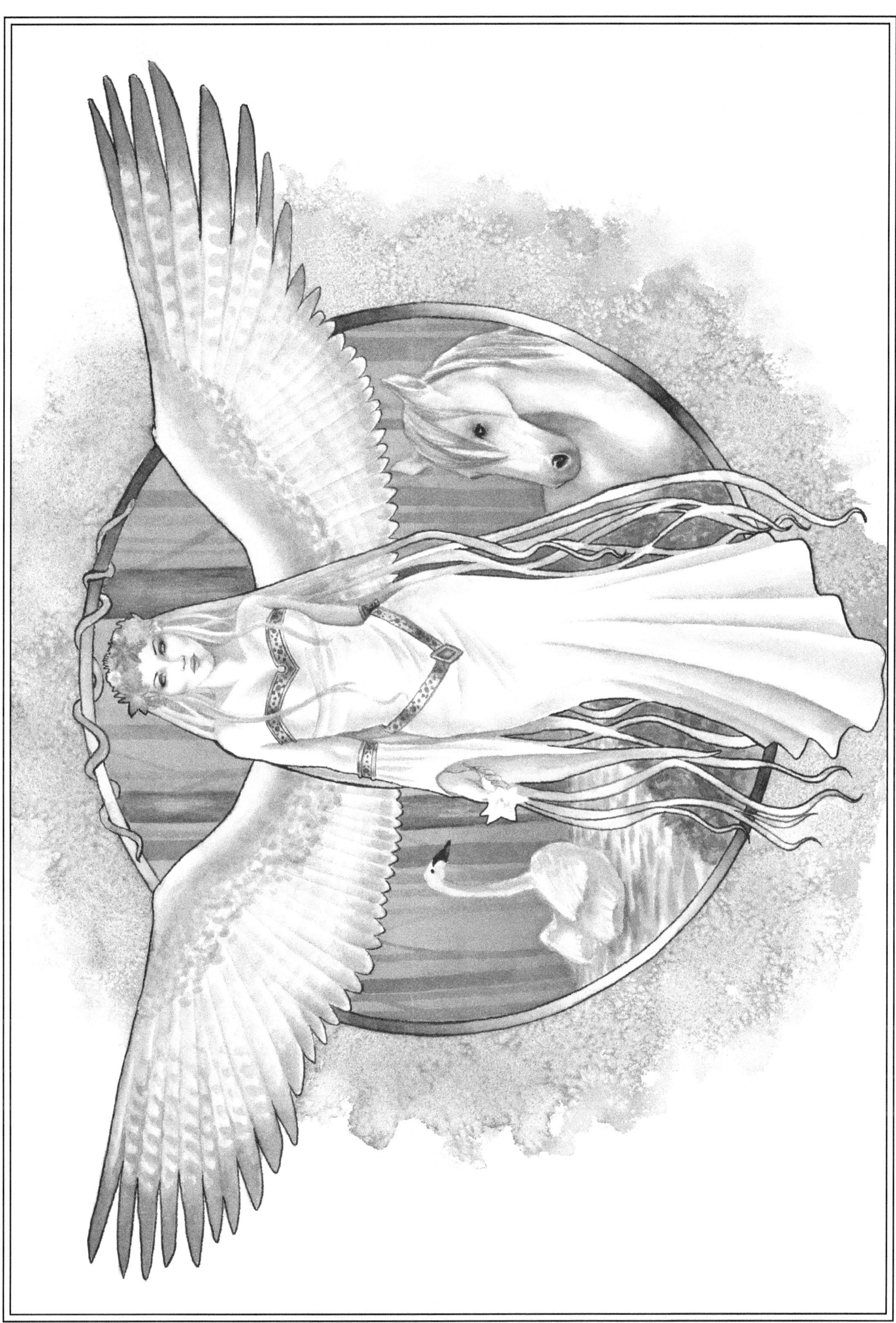

"Warm my Heart"

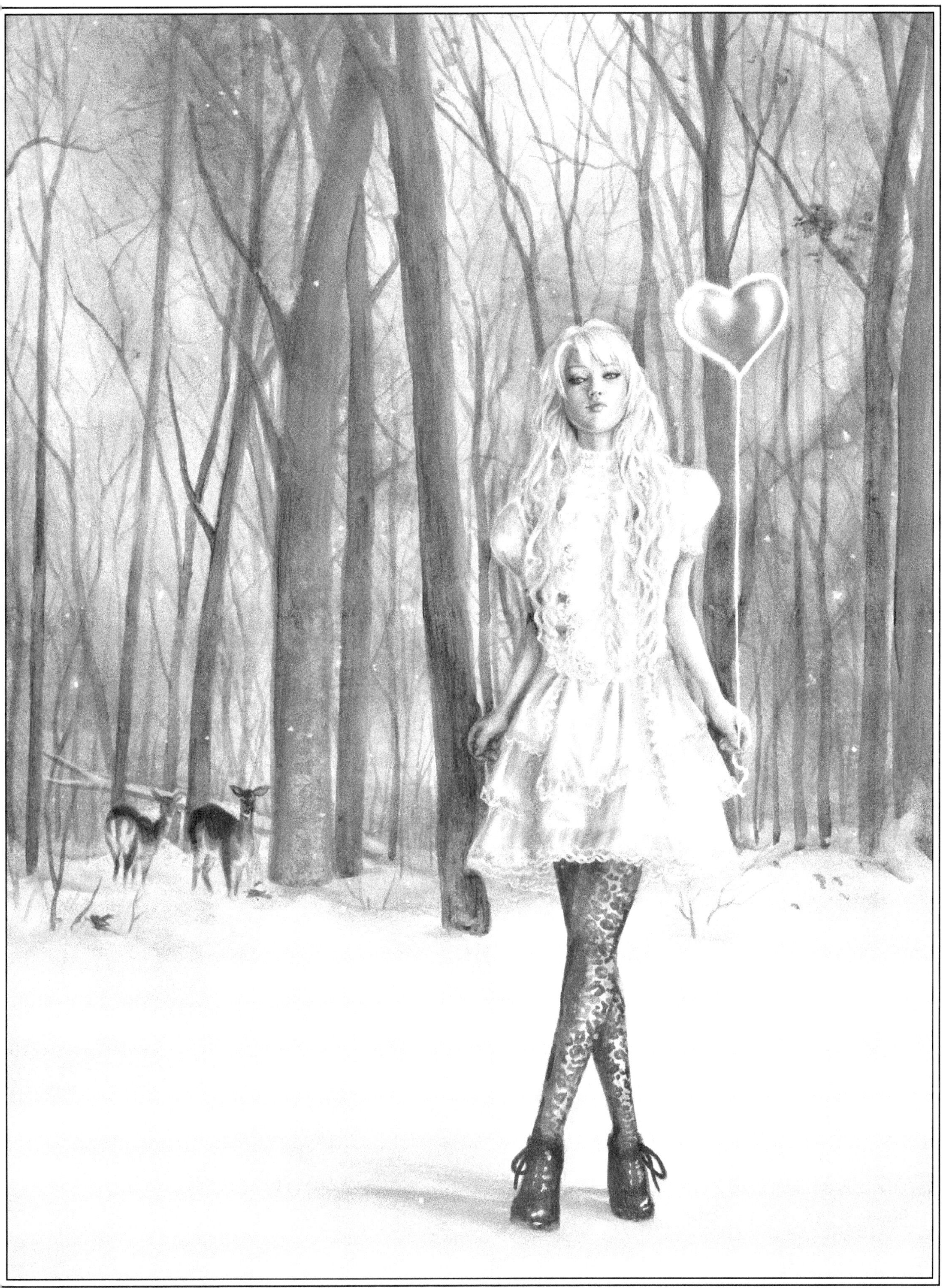

"Wandering Through The Woods"

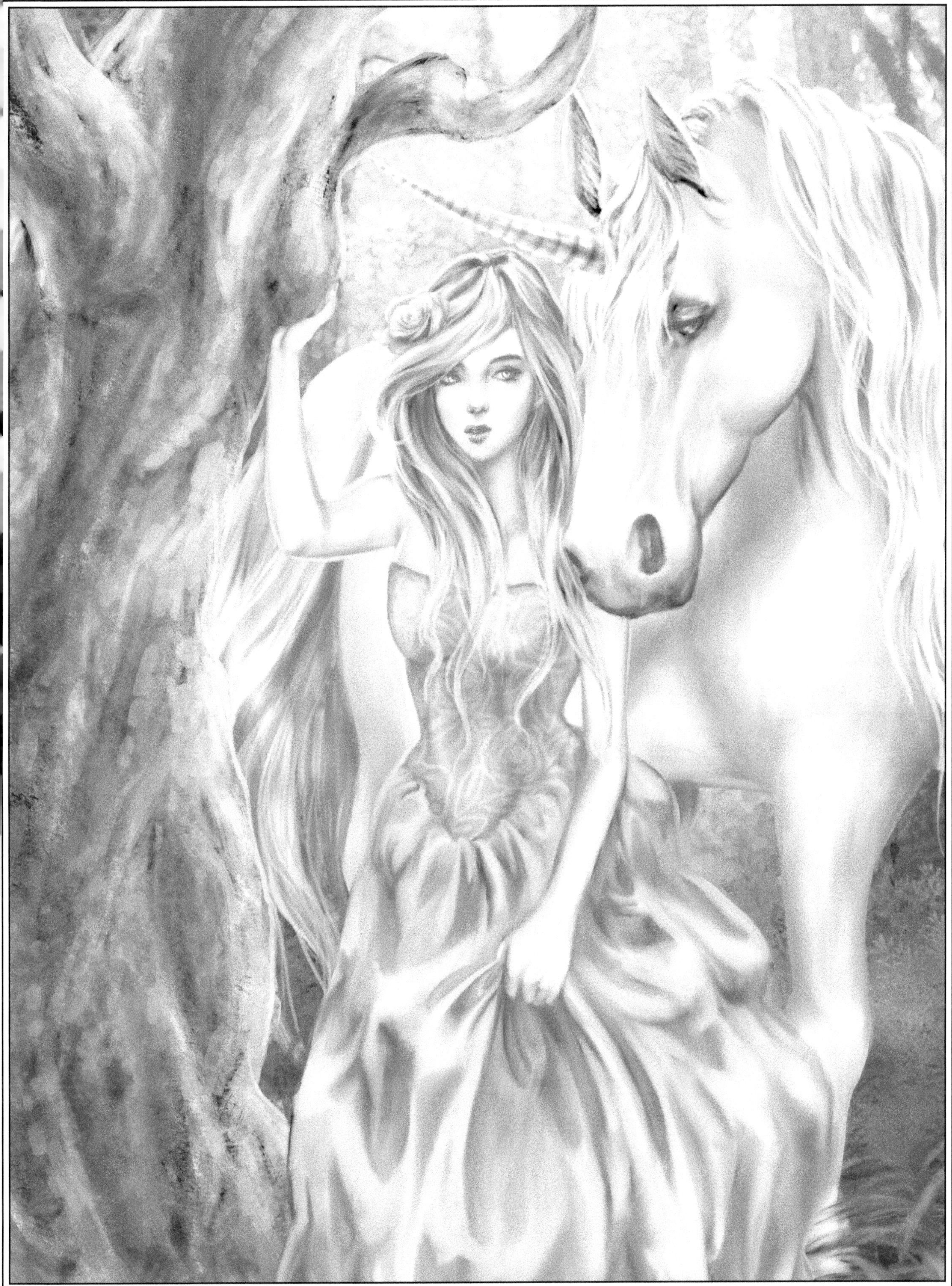

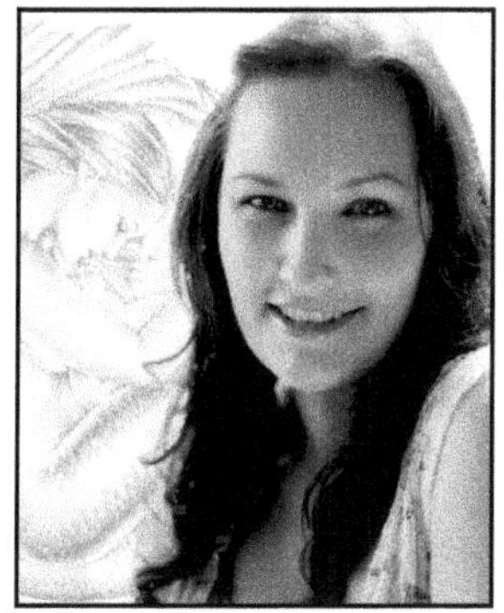

About the Artist

As a lover of all things fantasy, Selina has made a living as an artist since she was 23 years old selling her magical creations. Her works range from oil paintings to oracle decks, dolls to digital scrapbooking, plus Young Adult novels, jewelry, and coloring books.

Born in 1981 to Australian and Maltese parents, Selina lives in Australia with her husband and daughter. She loves food, gardening, geekery and all things magical.

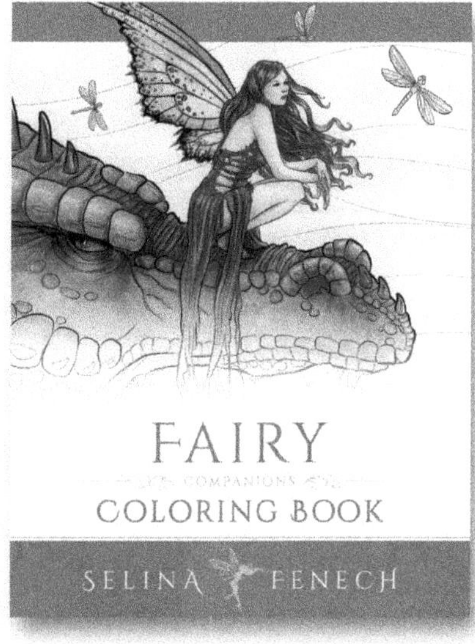

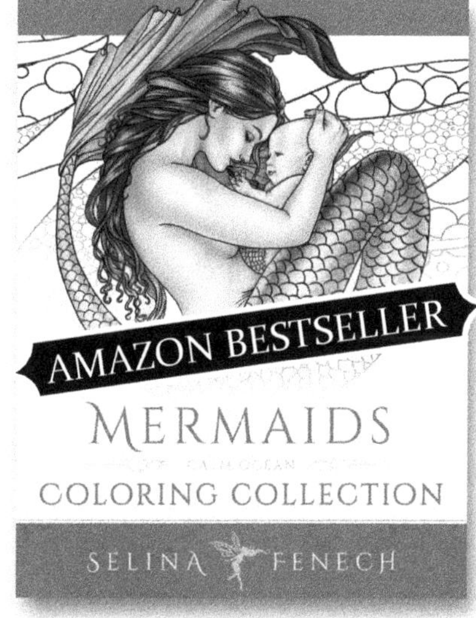

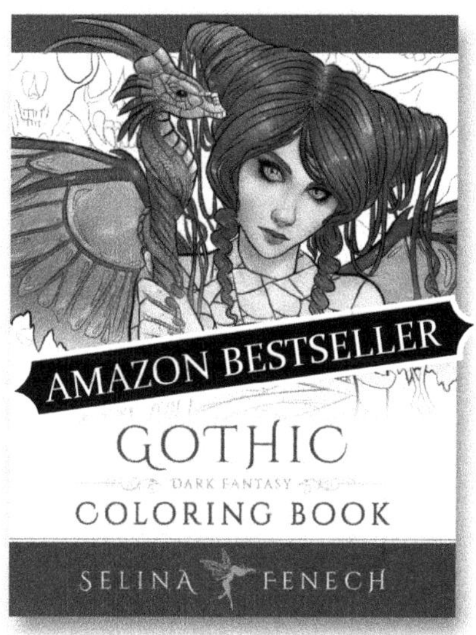

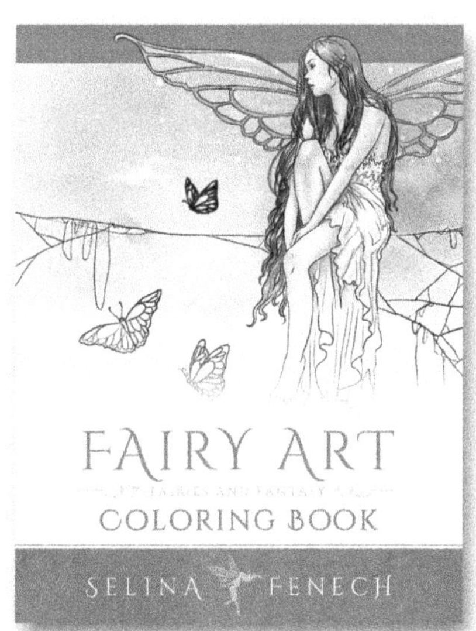

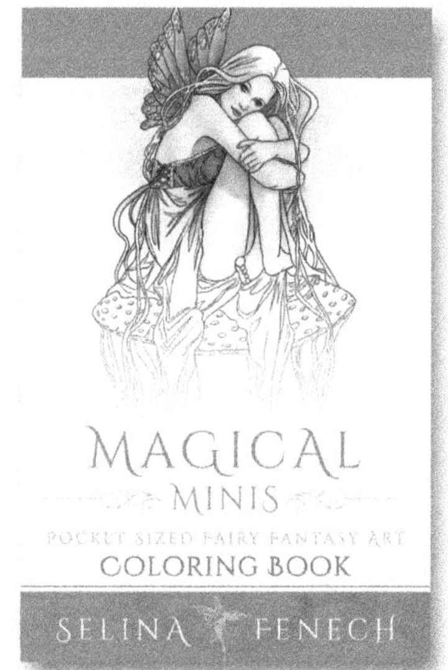

See all books online at - viewAuthor.at/sfcolor

Share Your Work

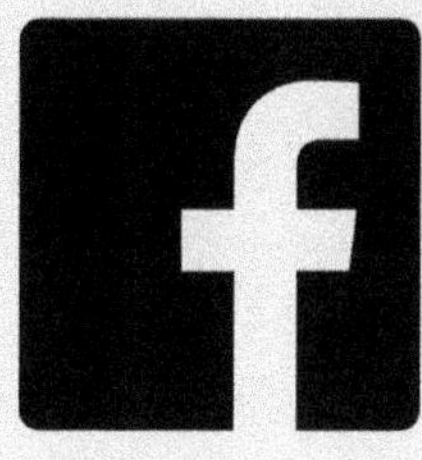

Share on Instagram with **#colorselina** to be included in Selina's coloring gallery, and visit the gallery for inspiration.

selinafenech.com/coloringgallery

www.ingramcontent.com/pod-product-compliance
Ingram Content Group UK Ltd.
Pitfield, Milton Keynes, MK11 3LW, UK
UKHW051207260726
13967UKWH00011B/3148